Redesigning Work

'A intelligent, deeply thoughtful book that will walk you through the choices that will be critical to your people's future happiness and well-being, and by extension, to your organization's performance. Lynda Gratton's sharp new book gives us a practical approach to parsing out the choices that will work in our unique situations'
Rita McGrath, bestselling author and professor at Columbia Business School

'We are going through a period of extraordinary change. Technology, climate and social. Working practices will change profoundly and the impact on working habits will be significant, affecting every employee and employer. This is a must-read for both, as Lynda's book helps us think through the implications'
Lord Mervyn Davies of Abersoch, former CEO and Chairman of Standard Chartered

'I have always been struck by Lynda's vast thinking about the future of work. Lynda's broad approach to researching the many ways we live and work (beyond the tech paradigm of remote work) is now the likely key to stabilizing our path to the future. *Redesigning Work* will be a hit'
John Maeda, American executive, designer and technologist

'Lynda's book couldn't come at a better time as every CEO and their senior team grapple with the future of work. It's unlikely that companies will immediately know the best way to change, which is why Lynda's practical advice will be highly valued by the business world. I am very excited by the possibility of a better working world and I think this book provides excellent advice as we attempt to build it!'
Ann Cairns, Vice Chairman, Mastercard

'*Redesigning Work* seizes the once-in-a-lifetime opportunity to rethink not only where work takes place (virtual, hybrid), but also who works (changing demographics), what we do (evolving tasks), how we work (collaboration), and why we work (purpose and impact). Gratton draws on her extensive experience and expertise to create a well-honed field guide and four-step process that will guide you and your teams to thrive in the future as it rapidly emerges and morphs around. *Redesigning Work* is the ultimate guide for those of us championing team human'
Heather E. McGowan, future of work strategist, keynote speaker and author of *The Adaptation Advantage*

'Lynda Gratton uses the insight that the pandemic has already shaken us out of our old ways of working to show us how to use this opportunity to fix many problems with the way we work now. An extremely timely and useful book'
Peter Cappelli, author of *The Future of the Office: Work from Home, Remote Work, and the Hard Choices We All Face*

'Lynda Gratton has increasingly set herself apart from the pack; she is now the lead thinker helping us interpret the changing face of business. This is a book that has helped summarize the changed world we face, and also to make sense of it'
Bruce Daisley, bestselling author and former Vice President of Twitter

'A book the "future of work" has been waiting for. Lynda Gratton's *Redesigning Work* is not only chock-full of astute insights and crystal clear realities, it contains a purposeful playbook to right so much of what has gone wrong in our workplaces'
Dan Pontefract, leadership strategist and bestselling author of *Lead. Care. Win.* and *Flat Army*

'A remarkably thoughtful and practical guide to rethinking how work gets done. Perhaps the only thing we know for sure is that the workplace of the future is a moving target that will continue to come into focus in the coming years, influenced by many voices and many factors. With Gratton's help, this journey can be far more systematic and rewarding than it would otherwise be'
Amy C. Edmondson, professor, Harvard Business School and author of *The Fearless Organization* (Wiley, 2019)

'This is a hugely insightful and timely guide for everyone challenged about how to redesign work in a thoroughly reimagined future. The strong focus on people, talent and potential is particularly valuable. This overall rigorous approach can work for organizations of any operational size, scale or sector'
Dame Mary Marsh, non-executive director of HSBC Bank and member of the governing body at London Business School

'Redesigning work is complex and extremely challenging. Drawing on decades of research and practice, and very timely current case studies, Gratton provides a tour de force treatment of a mission-critical issue for organizations everywhere'
Alec Levenson, Senior Research Scientist, Center for Effective Organizations, Marshall School of Business, University of Southern California

'*Redesigning Work* is an invaluable guidebook for every leader and organization, with its practical frameworks and can-do examples of how to apply bold thinking on where and when work gets done. The author shows how we will increase human potential at work, reimagining a future of work that attracts the workers of the future. This is a must-read for every leader interested in seizing the post pandemic opportunities by unleashing their human capital in new ways!'
Jonas Prising, Chairman and CEO of ManpowerGroup

'Immediately applicable recommendations for organizations and more importantly, people, to redesign a better way of working together. A must-read'
Selina Millstam, VP & Global Head of Talent Management, Ericsson

'The future of work is an active and crucial discussion in organizations around the world. Lynda's book is a brilliant provocation to help challenge perceptions, habits and priorities, and help us all create workplaces that provide good work that benefits individuals, businesses and the economy'
Andy Briggs, Group CEO of Phoenix Group and former chair of the ABI

'Everyone is talking about the future of work. This book provides practical insight on how to respond to challenges such as automation and working from home with examples from organizations around the world. Indispensable reading for everyone interested in how we will work in future'
Minouche Shafik, author of *What We Owe Each Other* and director of the London School of Economics

'Thought-provoking, deeply researched and invaluable, this fascinating book will help you build, lead and guide your organization through this time of extraordinary change'
Gary Hamel, founder of Strategos and management expert

'Wow!!! Linda has done it again!! With extraordinary insights, captivating stories and relevant tools, she has characterized the future of work. Her four-step logic and sixteen actions will be a blueprint for any individual and organization folding the future into the present'
Dave Ulrich, Rensis Likert Professor, Ross School of Business, University of Michigan Partner, The RBL Group

Lynda Gratton is one of the foremost global thought-leaders on the future of work, named by 'Business Thinkers 50' as one of the top fifteen business thinkers and described as a 'rock star' teacher. Lynda is Professor of Management Practice at London Business School, where she received the 'teacher of the year' award and designed and directs 'the future of work' elective, one of the school's most popular electives. Her research on hybrid work was featured as the cover article for *Harvard Business Review* in May 2021 and she explores issues of work in her MIT Sloan column. Over a decade ago Lynda founded HSM-Advisory, which has supported more than ninety companies around the world to future-proof their business strategy. Her ten books, including *The 100-Year Life*, have sold over a million copies and been translated into more than fifteen languages. Lynda serves as a Fellow of the World Economic Forum and co-chairs the WEF Council on Work, Wages and Job Creation. Lynda has sat on the advisory board of Japan's Prime Minister Abe and serves on the advisory board of a number of global companies.

Lynda's website: www.lyndagratton.com

Lynda's company website: www.hsm-advisory.com

Redesigning Work

How to Transform Your Organization and Make Hybrid Work for Everyone

LYNDA GRATTON

BUSINESS

PENGUIN BUSINESS

UK | USA | Canada | Ireland | Australia
India | New Zealand | South Africa

Penguin Business is part of the Penguin Random House group of companies
whose addresses can be found at global.penguinrandomhouse.com.

Penguin
Random House
UK

First published 2022
001

Copyright © Lynda Gratton, 2022

The moral right of the author has been asserted

Set in 12/14.75 pt Dante MT Std
Typeset by Jouve (UK), Milton Keynes
Printed and bound in Great Britain by Clays Ltd, Elcograf S.p.A.

The authorized representative in the EEA is Penguin Random House Ireland,
Morrison Chambers, 32 Nassau Street, Dublin D02 YH68

A CIP catalogue record for this book is available from the British Library

ISBN: 978-0-241-55818-8

Follow us on LinkedIn: https://www.linkedin.com/company/penguin-connect/

www.greenpenguin.co.uk

MIX
Paper from
responsible sources
FSC® C018179

Penguin Random House is committed to a
sustainable future for our business, our readers
and our planet. This book is made from Forest
Stewardship Council® certified paper.

To all those who are bold enough to redesign work

Contents

List of Figures

Introduction

We are experiencing what is undoubtedly the greatest global shift in work for a century. It's come at a time when much was already transforming: automation was reshaping industries and changing our jobs; we were coming to terms with living longer than our parents and potentially working into our seventies; and many people were experiencing at first hand how traditional family and community structures had become more diverse.[1] Our needs and what we wanted from work and from companies had already dramatically shifted.

But many companies had not responded fast enough to these changing needs. Long before the arrival of the pandemic, we knew we'd got into bad working habits: scheduling too many meetings, putting up with long commutes, not spending enough time with our families and feeling the pressure to be 'always on'. These were common complaints that we've long said we wish could be fixed. The wear and tear on our mental health and our increasing carbon footprint warned us our way of working was wrong. But these working habits were deeply ingrained and hard to shift. Then the global pandemic hit in March 2020 and changed everything.

Our collective experience of the pandemic created a once-in-a-lifetime opportunity to rethink what we want from work and our working lives. We had a chance to question many fundamental assumptions, adopt new habits and form new narratives of how work gets done. The experience also confronted corporate leadership teams with the challenge of how they would respond. Would they stay with their ways of working or would they use this as an opportunity to be bold and redesign work to make working a more purposeful, productive, agile and flexible activity?

This is an extraordinary opportunity to redesign work. My aspiration is to support you and your colleagues in this endeavour – to understand and take account of the technological, demographic and social trends that are shaping work, and to learn from what the pandemic has taught us. Whether you are leading a team of five people, a company of twenty or a multinational employing thousands, this book will help you choose how you work and what your team and business can become.

Redesigning Work is a culmination of my research and teaching on work, and my insights from the industry leaders I advise. The experiences of the pandemic accelerated and brought renewed impetus to The Future of Work Consortium, the research initiative I launched in 2010 which has brought together executives from over ninety companies to debate and share ideas about work. These ideas had been translated into action through my research and advisory practice HSM Advisory, which has partnered with many organizations in their journey of redesigning work. As a professor at London Business School I created in 2015 an MBA elective, The Future of Work, which has given me an opportunity to hear the perspectives of the thousands of students I've taught and fine tune my own thinking. I've also, from March 2020, kept a daily journal (running to twenty volumes) in which I note what I have witnessed during the pandemic. It is clear to me there has never been a better time to act.

This book is fundamentally a call to action. To cultivate and trial new ideas, to listen to new perspectives and, crucially, to make the leap from the *rhetoric* of ideas to the *action* of creation and implementation. And to help you make that leap successfully, I have created a playbook to support you and your organization on your journey of redesigning work.

This is a chance to harness the real momentum for a radical shift in how we work. Our growing confidence with working digitally and the sense of liberation we are feeling is propelling us forward into new habits, and every day we are more forgetful of how we worked before. We are changing and our work is changing.

From 'freeze' to 'unfreeze' to 'refreeze'

The impact of the pandemic has been extraordinary and cannot be overstated. To help describe some of the monumental changes it set into motion, we can look to psychologist Kurt Lewin, whose 'freeze, unfreeze' model represents the process of institutional change.[2] He described how under normal conditions organizations are 'frozen' or in a state of 'freeze'. Their culture, structure (such as who reports to whom), practices (like who gets paid what) and processes (such as recruitment) are fixed. But this stasis can begin to change when faced with an external threat. These threats can take many forms: a new competitor comes to market, customers become dissatisfied with the product or service, or a tranche of talented employees leave. At this point, the company transforms from 'freeze' to 'unfreeze'. Structures become unstable, executives begin to question long-held assumptions and they experiment with new ways of operating. The result is that the institution begins to change. But, over time as the threat diminishes, the company begins to 'refreeze' and the period of innovation and change settles back into stasis and stability.

Before the pandemic, faced with automation as well as demographic and social shifts, some companies had already begun to 'unfreeze'. They had realized that automation would require employees to rapidly upskill or even reskill to completely different roles, and that this would put learning at a premium. They had understood that, faced with the possibility of such a long working life, the traditional three-stage career path of full-time education, full-time work and retirement was ill equipped, and instead a 'multi-stage' working life was now more appropriate. Which meant that employees would value the opportunity to dip in and out of work, to start a business on the side, go back to education or travel the world. And as family structures morphed, so they acknowledged this diversity and began to design processes that would make their company an attractive place to work – for everyone.

And as these executives learnt more about automation and these demographic and social shifts they realized that, fundamentally, work that enabled flexibility was both more desirable and, if intentionally designed, also more productive. So they had begun to engage in creating this flexibility by 'unfreezing' job structures, reward mechanisms and so on. They had begun the journey illustrated in Figure 1.

Some moved their practices upwards along the vertical axis towards greater flexibility of *place*, trialling home, remote or shared-space working for particular types of worker. As early as the 1980s British Telecom, now BT, adopted homeworking for call-centre staff.

Others pushed along the horizontal axis, experimenting with *time*, testing compressed hours, encouraging part-time working, enabling employees to take an hour off in the morning and work an extra hour in the afternoon or share their role with another person. There is much we can learn from these early adopters, and in this book I will share some of these insights.

Yet for many companies, their experiments with flexible place and time working were small scale, and leaders and executives resisted change on a larger scale. They remained in the 'freeze' state.

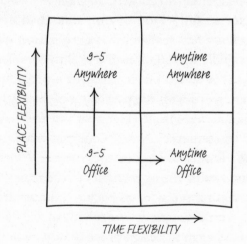

Figure 1: Time and place flexibility.

In March 2020 the pandemic initiated a global 'unfreeze' of a scale and velocity previously impossible to imagine. Hundreds of millions of workers switched to remote working as countries all over the world entered lockdown. Many more millions compressed their hours around looking after children, sick relatives or those in their community. Companies had to innovate at a rapid pace to keep their workers safe and remain operational. Experiments in time and place were being played out in businesses in almost every country of the world. This was 'unfreeze' on a monumental scale.

Whilst some executive teams had experimented with being flexible around time and place, now every executive team was faced with a new reality. Could they extend their ideas of place to include working from anywhere (most often the home); could they extend their ideas of time from nine-to-five to something more flexible – and, importantly, what role could technology play in boosting virtual connectivity in a world that was becoming less physically connected by the day?

In normal circumstances each company, when it experiences 'unfreeze', does so in its own time and in a way that reflects its unique context. But in the pandemic, companies all round the world were simultaneously experiencing the conditions that lead to 'unfreeze'. This was a *collective experience*. Leaders who rarely talked about time and place were making predictions about the role of the office, or the mental health of their employees, whilst commentators of all kinds, business psychologists, technologists and journalists, were weighing in with their perspective. The collective 'unfreeze' gave way to *collective imagination*. Social media was full of people imagining what working from home could be and reimagining the office. And leaders, disconnected from the normal communication structures like 'town hall' meetings, now took to remote communication platforms and virtual meetings to address the workforce, often from their own homes.

This collective experience also became a *collective journey* as executives looked to their employees, their teams and their peers in other companies to get a sense of the emerging reality and their options. One executive I'd been in touch with throughout the period of the pandemic was Leanne Cutts, who was at the time Group Chief Marketing Officer at the global bank HSBC, which operates across more than sixty markets. As she explained to me in June 2021:

> We are certainly still at the unfreeze stage. Parts of the businesses have made decisions about the broad principles of the redesign of work, others are still thinking these through. I call these 'wet clay' – we are still playing with options and we are far from solidi- fied. I'd prefer we had watery feet than lack imagination – this is a real opportunity to raise the bar, to really lift up.

Raising the bar

The pandemic has presented the unique opportunity to 'raise the bar' and 'really lift up' in part because it removed institutional lag, or the delay between institutions and businesses implementing the changes that individuals want and need. That's partly a result of the agile capabilities created by new digital skills and the dismantling of bureaucracy. But I believe it's more than this. It also reflects how business leaders themselves are feeling and what they are motivated by to achieve change.

Many leaders began to sound more empathic to others and their circumstances than ever before. That's certainly reflected in issues about the tensions between work and home, which frankly have been around for decades. What was lacking was the power to do much about these tensions. What has changed is that during lock- down leaders experienced these tensions first hand.

Of course, it's not that a senior executive in a large house with a garden had the same experience as a single mother in a small apartment lacking outside space, or indeed the same experience as many employees within their company. For many leaders, their previous experience had been shielded from the everyday realities of their employees. Some had nannies to help with childcare, or cleaners or gardeners to take care of household chores. Faced with these support systems, many were ignorant of the everyday lives of others. But the pandemic did – at least during 2020 and much of 2021 – lift what philosopher John Rawls in the 1970s described as a 'veil of ignorance'.[3] Thanks to a variety of quarantines, lockdowns and work-from-home orders, leaders began to experience more viscerally the stresses and strains that others experience. And for many leaders that's created a sense of understanding and empathy they'd previously lacked.

The result is that leaders are now more motivated to put their shoulders to the wheels of both quick wins and long-term changes. Importantly, as leaders have themselves become involved with change – which affects them as intimately as it does their employees – they are ever more aware of the trade-offs. They are realizing at a visceral level that, whilst the office might be a great place for face-to-face cooperation, those long commutes and hours spent behind a desk deplete energy. Or, whilst creating schedules when colleagues can work together increases coordination, it can often break concentration and lead to endless Zoom meetings.

We are all discovering that, whilst solving a single problem brings instant gratification, it also brings trade-offs. This is a moment when all these trade-offs are finally on the table for tough discussion. And these tough discussions are crucial because we are beginning to understand what economic historians have observed from 1800 right up to the present time. That new technologies and ways of working rarely bring the anticipated productivity advantage unless and until they are combined with best-practice organizational techniques.[4] And moreover, that the necessary types of organizational shift have historically proceeded very slowly. Until now . . .

In the spring of 2020 Hiroki Hiramatsu, the head of global HR at the Japanese technology company Fujitsu, and his executive team moved almost all their 60,000 Tokyo-based employees from office to home in less than two weeks. He said to me at the time:

We are not going back. We are never going back to everybody going into the office every day. We normally spend two hours a day to commute. These two hours are kind of wasting time. We can use these two hours for education, training, family care. What we need to think about is how to make our own life work productive and creative. We need more ideas to make remote work effective.

He was not alone – across every country of the world executive teams were doing the same. Yet, whilst at any point in time the future is unpredictable, I began to realize that for many executives the pandemic had taught them a great deal – that people can learn digital skills fast, bureaucracy can be dismantled effectively, and that flexing place is possible for many. And along the way they learnt about the negative consequences – that the pressure to be 'always on' is tough, and that human networks and connections matter in ways they hadn't fully recognized.

Here are some of the new-found realities that organizations are drawing from as they think about positively building from the collective experience of the pandemic and redesigning work.

We accelerated digital skills

My research with executives produces a recurring complaint: that the workforce is too slow to learn new skills, particularly digital skills. But, during the pandemic, we were all forced to become 'digital natives' in the way we worked, learnt, bought stuff and socialized. In the early months of the pandemic Jeff Maggioncalda, CEO of the online education platform Coursera, explained to me, 'Enrolment in China, Japan and Italy is up by over 300 per cent, with courses on public health dominating.' What was exciting to him was the way in which these online learners were supporting each other. 'There has been an amazing amount of sharing, for example, "How do you run a virtual class?" It's a new spirit of accepting new things.'

More was to come. The number of students and teachers

using Google Classroom doubled in two months to 100 million. The company reported a 'massive increase' in sales of Google-designed Chromebooks, the laptop of choice for many schools, and time spent on the internet company's Meet video app, used by students as well as workers, was up thirty-fold. Ramkumar Chandrasekaran, who heads up human resources for the UK in the Mumbai-headquartered technology company TCS (Tata Consultancy Services), told me that from early 2020 to 2021 the number of learning hours in the UK logged by employees increased by a significant 60 per cent. It's no surprise that Satya Nadella, the CEO of Microsoft, believes that our experience of the pandemic fast-forwarded the adoption of a wide range of new technologies by two years. With their new-found confidence, many executives jumped into digital experiments. Anne Sheehan, who leads the UK business of the global telecoms company Vodafone, described to me how they had boosted their experiments with VR cameras to demonstrate to customers their new technologies. Peter Brown, head of human resources for Europe for the professional services group PwC, shared how the firm used immersive virtual reality to help their new graduates learn about the company in their first few weeks.

As we go about redesigning work these new-found digital skills will become crucial. Inevitably, as work becomes more remote and virtual, a whole host of new processes including digital scheduling, project management and digital collaboration will become the norm. The digital skills that are being developed now will play a crucial role in these process innovations.

We threw bureaucracy on the 'bonfire'

Many executive teams seized the opportunity to ditch ways of working that had historically slowed them down. Early in the pandemic, one telecoms CEO told me, 'We've thrown bureaucracy out of the window, we moved 6,000 employees to work from home in four days.' Another said, 'It was all remarkably smooth, the clock speed increased. We were ruthless in our prioritization – we dumped 20 per cent of what we do immediately – decluttered.' Anne Shee-han, at Vodafone, told me:

> My team used to take a full day out for a strategy discussion. We now break it up into two-and-a-half-hour sessions. It's very clear what we're going to discuss, the pre-read gives us time to think, we know what we want to achieve. We have shorter sessions with a clearer outcome. This is really working for us.

Stanford professor Nicholas Bloom describes this prioritiza-tion, decluttering and outcome focus as 'a bonfire of unnecessary regulations'.[5]

Of course, bureaucracy has a tendency to creep back as hier-archies reform and meetings start to proliferate. But as they go about redesigning work, many executives are being super sensitive to this and laying down practices and processes that continue to stream-line ways of working to ensure that the company stays agile and adaptive. By, for example, significantly reducing hierarchical levels, creating more agile working groups and limiting the numbers of meetings.

We better understood the payoff and challenges of true 'flexibility'

Flexibility, and being truly responsive to the individual needs of their employees, is often on the wish list for the executives I interview for my research on the future of work. Yet they also told me how they found it hard to move from the rhetoric of flexibility to the reality of putting it into practice. Then the pandemic cre-ated a chance to create a stronger alignment between rhetoric and reality.

Many executives began to see that working flexibly was possible for most workers. For Hiromasa-san from Fujitsu the benefits of being more flexible and adaptive were showing within a few months of lockdown. He told me at the time:

We want to attract people with different skill sets and experience. Three years ago, only female employees worked from home, many had caring responsibilities. But in this new situation everyone can now work from home. From my own experiences, I now understand what the female employees had told me. My hope is that this Work Life Shift will help to retain our female talent. Also, now we are working anywhere, anytime, this allows more collaboration with people outside of Fujitsu, with other people in other companies.

Martin Sorrell, the advertising boss who runs S4 Capital, summed it up for many leaders when he said he found working from home 'energizing', and expected it to herald a 'permanent change' to his working practices. In view of this he had already started ending leases at some sites. 'I spend around £35 million on property in a year, I'd much rather invest that in people than expensive offices.'

This provides a real opportunity to move away from inflexible office-based working practices to embrace more flexible ways of working – in terms not only of place but also of time.

We learnt we need to respect the 'off' switch

It turns out that a more flexible way of working has one significant side-effect; we are constantly connected. Ramkumar Chandrasekaran from TCS summarized this perfectly to me when he said, 'People are spending ridiculously long hours in front of their computers and the main reason is there are way too many team meetings. Because it is so easy for people to make these meetings they are going ahead and doing it.'

The emotional and physical toll of this began to become more obvious as the pandemic progressed. Ramkumar continued, 'In part it's a result of the time gains from no longer commuting. It turned out that many people reallocated these "extra hours" back to work, and in doing so they worked longer hours.'

Just how long is clear from the aggregate time data on email traffic collected during the pandemic in the US and Europe from over three million people. What this data showed is that the span of working time (defined by the first and last email in a twenty-four-hour period) increased by 48.5 minutes, from 9 hours 51.5 minutes to 10 hours 40 minutes (that's an extra 8.2 per cent).[6] And that's partly because of an increase in emails sent after business hours.

During the pandemic, many people struggled with finding the 'off' switch – and, as I will show, creating a purposeful way of working that builds in time for focus will be crucial to the productive flow of work. That's going to be a real challenge as you go about redesigning work, and the success of any redesign will be judged in part on this.

We realized that human connections really matter

The experience of many people working longer hours was visible to most executive teams. What was less visible, but became ever more salient, was the unexpected impact of homeworking on people's networks. In general, networks shrank. That's because people working from home spent more time with those they already knew well, less time with people they knew less well, and created far fewer new friendships.

We came to understand that when everyone works from home, we lose face-to-face or 'water cooler' conversations. Andy Haldane, then chief economist at the Bank of England, explained:

> Exposure to new and different experiences – sounds, smells, environments, ideas, people – is a key source of creative spark. These external stimuli are fuel for our imaginations and the imagined, made real, is what we typically mean by creativity. Homeworking can starve us of many of these creative raw ingredients – the chance conversation, the new person or idea or environment. Homeworking means serendipity is supplanted by scheduling, face-to-face by Zoom.[7]

But have we been overestimating the benefits of face to face at a time when our digital capabilities have increased? That's the view of Leigh Thompson at Northwestern University: 'Based on research I and others have conducted over the past couple of decades, I believe that the shift to remote work actually has the potential to improve group creativity and ideation, despite diminished in-person communication.'[8] As we will explore, some executive teams have put themselves on a fast learning curve on how to innovate in a virtual environment.

Yet whilst there was greater insight into how to innovate virtually, there was also growing awareness of the needs of a specific group of people. We learnt that lack of face-to-face connectivity was particularly tough for young people as they joined companies without being around people in an office environment. We asked: how do they learn about what the job is, what is expected of them, and how they need to behave without the opportunity to observe their colleagues and absorb subtle cues?

This realization of the importance of human connections is apparent in the way that executives are now thinking more deeply about networks structures and how knowledge flows across the company. In Chapter 2, 'Understand', we will take a much closer look at networks and how they can be understood and shaped.

The time is now

Our collective experience of the pandemic has created a once-in-a-lifetime opportunity to rethink what the workers among us want from work and our working lives and what those of us who are leaders want to encourage and institute within our organizations. We've had a chance to question many fundamental assumptions, adopt new habits, and form new narratives of how work gets done. We've learnt many vital lessons from this time of 'unfreeze'. We are now faced with some significant choices – do we go back to our old ways of working or do we use this as an opportunity to completely redesign work and make it more purposeful, productive and fulfilling for all?

In facing these choices, there are questions of purpose and capabilities to be explored. What is the company purpose that you want to enhance through redesigning work, and how will redesigning work support your values and enhance productivity? And with regard to capabilities, what are the capabilities that you need to develop now that will enable your company to meet this purpose – in terms of both individual human capabilities and machine capabilities?

Drawing from my own research and advisory experience, I have created a design process to support you in answering these questions about purpose and capabilities. It takes you and your team through four steps: understanding people, networks and jobs; reimagining work; modelling and testing your redesign ideas; and acting on your models and creating new ways of working.

This design process is crucial because, in my experience, a 'one-size-fits-all' approach will not work. Instead you have the opportunity to create a way of working that fully resonates with your unique purpose and values, that acknowledges the capabilities and motivations of your employees and that ultimately increases productivity and fulfilment. This is your corporate 'signature'. To help you write it I've brought frameworks and insights from my own and others' research, and insights from companies across the world who are also embarking on this journey and who are learning fast how to redesign work.

To guide you on this four-step design process, in this book I have created a Redesigning Work Playbook that you can share with your colleagues – you can also download it now at www.hsm-advisory.com/redesigning-work.

1. *How to Redesign Work*

Building a blueprint for your company's future will be an experience unique to you, and different for every company. You can create this unique signature by engaging in a four-step design process.

How best to redesign work? I've seen leaders and executive teams approaching this redesign in a top-down, hierarchical way; others have decided to leave the process entirely in the hands of individual managers. My experience is that neither works satisfactorily. Here's why: your business is a complex system with many moving parts. Top-down works only when leaders know exactly how to do this – and most don't. Yet leaving decisions to be made by individual managers can result in feelings of mistrust and unfairness across employee groups. The way you work and the way your business works is in need of a structural overhaul; your task is to guide that overhaul and develop a process of redesigning work that prepares everyone in the business for action.

To support you on this journey I have created a four-step process. The foundation of these four steps is my experiences as a researcher fascinated by networks, co-creation, fairness and the shifts (demographic, technological and societal) that shape work. Yet your journey has to be more than a research study, and to bring real insight and momentum I have studied, and in some cases advised, many executive teams. It is this combination of research frameworks and executive insights that will ensure that you and your team design work that is just right for you.

The four-step process for redesigning work

The four steps of the process for redesigning work are shown in Figure 2.

1. **Understand what matters.** Which skills, networks and jobs are crucial for productivity? How does knowledge flow within and across your business and what do these flows look like? What do your people want from work and from the company? How do people experience work across the whole of their employee life cycle?

2. **Reimagine the future.** From this foundation of rich understanding, you can start to devise optimal work designs. Imagine making the office a place of cooperation where conversation flows and people bump into each other in a serendipitous way. Or, imagine the home as a real source of healthy living and energy. Or imagine how focus and coordination can be supported by the ways that working time is structured.

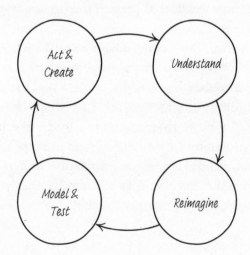

Figure 2. The four-step process for redesigning work.

3. **Model and test ideas.** Now these ideas can be modelled and tested against a number of factors that could be sources of risk. Is the model future-proofed? Will it still be relevant and purposeful in the short, medium and long term? Will the model of work both enable the technological transitions that are in play and, importantly, provide the support for employees to make the necessary skill transitions? And will the model be experienced as equitable and fair by employees across the company?

4. **Act on your model and create new ways of working.** This ensures the model of work will be embedded into the practices and culture of the company. To do that requires emphasizing the role of leaders and of the narratives and stories they tell. It means acknowledging and supporting the pivotal role of managers. And implementing widely a process of co-creation that engages people with the design choices and brings them along in the process of change.

Whilst I've ordered these steps 1 to 4 in a logical sequence, in reality any of the four-step cycle can be a point of entry. For example, some teams have jumped straight into reimagining work and then had to cycle back to understanding jobs, people and networks more deeply before progressing.

Developing your signature

One of the outcomes of the pandemic was a significant expansion of the choices about how, when and where people work. We learnt new habits, interacted more with technologies and changed our ways of working. We expanded our choices about place, and learnt it is possible to work from home, in a neighbourhood coffee shop, or in another country. We expanded our choices about time, and realized it is possible for some people to work three days in the office, take a sabbatical, work compressed hours, work four days a week and/or work on their own without connections to others. And we realized that when choices expand, so too does the combination of options.

Think of it this way: in 1908 when Henry Ford built his very first car, the Model T, his dream was to create a vehicle that was affordable, simple to operate and durable. This was the world's first mass-produced car. It was available in one model and in just one colour – black. Henry Ford was responding both to the constraints of the newly created assembly lines and the limited aspirations of car owners – who were so enchanted by the possibility of driving a motorized vehicle that the colour was of little consequence. Over time that single option became an array of enormous variety. Assembly-line production introduced the idea of modularity, so it became easier for manufacturers to create variety and individuality. And consumers, as they began to see that their own specific needs could be catered for, began to want to exercise choice. And choice and variety grew as more car manufacturers piled in, with their own unique designs.

Something similar is happening to working practices as a result of the pandemic. We've had, until now, what might be called the Model T Ford of work design, where work took place only in the office from 9 a.m. to 5 p.m. Both place and time (9 to 5) were constrained. That's the bottom left quadrant in Figure 1. Some executive teams were pushing to flexibility of time and place. But frankly, compared with what was to happen in March 2020 – this was just tinkering around the edges. It was still essentially the Model T Ford – just with a different coat of paint, or some snazzy upholstery. Few companies had fundamentally redesigned work.

Like car manufacturing was a century ago, we are at the beginning of an outpouring of variety. The shock of the pandemic created within many companies the momentum and energy to look again at values and purpose. To ask whether long-held assumptions still held, and to experiment with the extraordinary digital capacities that had developed as a consequence of being separated from the workplace.

Faced with these choices, executive teams began to describe paths forward that distinguished them from each other in ways they had not before. They began to imagine what could be their 'signature' – the unique or iconic ways of working that would attract and retain talent, boost productivity and support innovation. Developing that signature is every company's task and challenge – and opportunity – today.

Assemble your design team

As you embark on the four-step design process, this is a good time to ask yourself who can support you in your endeavour. As you will see from the case studies I share throughout the book, many design teams comprise cross-functional groups of differing competencies – capabilities such as employee experience, mobility, technology, human resources and business strategy. Is this the moment to reach out to others?

As noted in the Introduction, I have created a Redesigning Work Playbook to support you and your design team that can be downloaded from www.hsm-advisory.com, where you will also find a variety of other resources to support you.

As you go through this book you will find that the four design steps follow a logical process that takes you from understanding your company to moving into action. Along the way I've illustrated these steps through *insights* from companies who are engaged, like you, in the process of design. You will see that the issues of redesigning work are on the minds of executives from across the world – that's why you will find corporate insights drawn from many different countries including Australia, Canada, China, India, Japan, Sweden, the US and the UK. And you'll see that these design issues are relevant to a wide variety of industries – we'll hear specifically from companies in insurance, retail banking, telecoms, architecture and design, consumer goods and technology as well as organizations such as the Public Service Commission of New

South Wales in Australia. For each of the corporate insights I draw on, you'll find a set of 'questions for reflection'. These provide an opportunity for you and your colleagues to stand back and consider what you can learn from this company and what, if anything, you can bring into your own design thinking.

Describing these corporate insights are a series of *frameworks*. These are ways of looking at the issues I've used in my own thinking and practice as I go about teaching or advising companies on how to redesign work. I've spent a significant proportion of my adult life as a researcher – working closely with colleagues from my own and other academic institutions, and building models that help my students and the executives I advise to understand the world. I hope these frameworks will help you and your design team to understand your own company in terms of the way that work gets done and to collectively imagine what is possible for the future.

Let's get started.

2. Understand

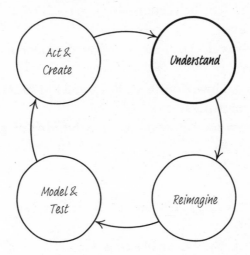

The design process begins with a foundation of deep understanding of your company's jobs and productive capabilities, people and their needs and experiences, networks and how knowledge flows. Without this deep understanding there's a risk that many of the new processes you come up with now will be viewed as a fad in a few years' time and be either buried or abandoned. Your work design will become a casualty if in the next few years it inadvertently erodes performance, or meddles with the natural channels of knowledge that, often unobserved, flow across the networks in a company, or enrages employees or makes them cross and disengaged because they feel they are being treated unfairly. That's why it is so crucial that as you embark on the redesign of work you understand what it is that enhances performance, how networks create strong knowledge flows, and what people want and will be engaged by.

To create a deep understanding of how your company works you will examine four topics with frameworks and corporate insights to guide how you and your colleagues think about the current reality. For each topic I'll share action points that will support you to put your redesign into action.

Understand: The behaviours and capabilities that support
   productivity
   – Framework: The four elements of productivity
   – Action #1
Understand: How knowledge flows and the structure of
   human networks
   – Framework: Networks and the diffusion of knowledge
   – Action #2
Understand: What people want from work and from the
   company
   – Framework: Talent and the desire for flexibility
   – Action #3
Understand: The experience of work
   – Insight: HSBC
   – Action #4

Understand: The behaviours and capabilities that support productivity

One of the major factors that will be used to judge the ultimate success of your model of work will be whether it enhances productivity. It does not need to have an immediate positive impact on productivity. Indeed, in the companies I have researched there is often an understanding that when a new way of working is introduced there will be a period of experimentation during which employees are learning and modifying and when productivity will dip. This was the case in the UK telecoms provider BT when it first introduced homeworking. However, this period of experimentation has a finite timeframe and over time executives will be asking whether these new ways of working enable and support employees to be more productive. In order to do that as you go about redesigning work you need to understand how best to leverage the behaviours and capabilities that support productivity.

This is not straightforward, in part because, unless you are in the smallest of businesses, there are many, many jobs within an organization, often vastly different from each other. So how do you go about redesigning work against this varied landscape? As you move later into the third step of the design process – 'Model and Test' – you will have a chance to look across the job spectrum to consider issues of fairness within it. For now, the focus is on understanding, and one way of understanding jobs is to think about them in broad categories – often called *job families*. These are jobs that have something in common. They could be call-centre jobs, or jobs that are customer facing, or jobs that are about managing people. As we take a closer look at how companies are redesigning work you will catch a glimpse of this variety.

So, begin by looking at the job families within your business. Start by choosing three job families to help you think through the variety and similarities. Then, for each job family, select one job and take a deep dive to understand it. Do this by looking at the *tasks* that together make up a job. Once you know something about what these tasks are, you will be in a good position to reimagine how you might support people to deliver these tasks productively.

To get a sense of this, take a look at your own job. What are the tasks you fulfil on a daily or weekly basis? A relatively complex job will involve around thirty tasks. In my own work, part of which is being a professor at London Business School, one task is teaching MBA students in ninety-minute lectures; another is running sixty-minute workshops with executives. I'm also responsible for marking student scripts, interviewing executives about their working practices to prepare cases, writing academic articles, preparing books, meeting with potential sponsors and so on. Like many of you there are various ways that I am productive.

The four elements of productivity

This job-deconstruction exercise will help you understand which elements of productivity to prioritize.

During the course of my research I have found that, whilst each job has its own groupings of tasks, there are four elements of productivity that most jobs are built around – energy, focus, coordination and cooperation (Figure 3). For each category I've outlined some of the positive and negative behaviours associated with each type of productivity.

> **Energy.** Many jobs have some tasks where people need to be energetic and animated when dealing with others, such as working on projects with tough deadlines, when keeping up the energy of team will be crucial, or being in meetings that require high levels of concentration and dynamism. Both these types of task need vitality and energy to deliver them. When people lack this energy they become fatigued in meetings and find it hard to meet deadlines. They find it tough to be productive and they become apathetic as their energy drains.

> **Focus.** There are jobs for which focus is essential. These tasks could include writing a report, looking at the transcripts from research interviews or examining

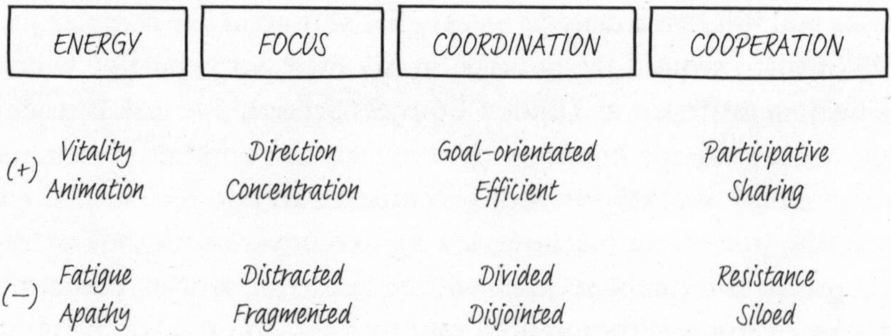

ENERGY	FOCUS	COORDINATION	COOPERATION
(+) Vitality Animation	Direction Concentration	Goal-orientated Efficient	Participative Sharing
(−) Fatigue Apathy	Distracted Fragmented	Divided Disjointed	Resistance Siloed

Figure 3. Framework: The elements of productivity.

data on a spreadsheet. They are ultimately tasks of concentration. When someone is distracted, or trying to multitask, then their concentration becomes scattered and their capacity to perform these tasks is diminished. Importantly, performing such tasks requires high-order cognitive functioning. And, as we will discover, these are tasks that require what neuroscientists call 'the rested brain'.

Coordination. Whilst focus is essentially an individual process, many of the tasks you and your colleagues perform are achieved through effective coordination with others. These include checking in with others, getting in-the-moment feedback, finding out what's on track in terms of project management and identifying where the problems are. When coordination is working well, people are fluidly aligning with each other and focusing on a shared goal – they are goal-orientated and efficient. When coordination breaks down it's not long before the teams become divided and disjointed and the project begins to flounder.

Cooperation. These are tasks where people are working together on new ideas and coming to new solutions. They are participative and sharing ideas with each other. These cooperative tasks could include working together in a multifunctional team on a new client pitch. They could be brainstorming a new product. When people come together in this cooperative way, the combination of ideas is powerful. When their different perspectives and knowledge combine there is the possibility of creating something that goes beyond the scope of any individual – to be truly creative and innovative. Yet when cooperation fails, people begin to lose trust in each other, they become resistant to others' ideas and the groups become siloed.

So, as you begin the step of understanding – work with your design team on these Action #1 bullet points:

Action #1
Understand the behaviours and capabilities that support productivity

- You can deepen your understanding by first identifying within your business a selection of at least three job families. These should be representative of the wider taxonomy of jobs that make up your business.
- Then taking each of these job families, look closely at the major tasks that make up one job. You will need to select from these the four or five tasks that are crucial to high performance.
- Against each of these tasks take a closer look at the four elements of the productivity framework (energy, focus, coordination, cooperation), and against each select those elements of productivity that are most crucial to the role.

Understand: How knowledge flows and the structure of human networks

This description of job tasks and the related element of productivity assumes an almost static process, which is essentially about the individual. In reality, people, the tasks they perform and the jobs they do are embedded within networks of human connections. It is through these connections that flow knowledge, insight and innovation. One of the major insights from the experience of the pandemic is how important these often-overlooked human connections are to organizational health and vitality.

It is important to understand networks and knowledge flows because any redesign of work can inadvertently disrupt them. It is no surprise that it's the potential disruption of networks and knowledge flows that is at the heart of two major concerns about the redesign of work: the socialization of the young and the possibility of serendipitous encounters. The fear that young joiners to a firm will suffer if they work from home as they will not be able to observe and network with more experienced members of the firm. And anxiety that the 'water cooler' conversations and the serendipitous encounters that happen when people simply bump into each other will be diminished. These concerns are real and valid – and so, before decisions about the redesign of work are taken, you need to have a view of the current structure of networks and knowledge flows and use this to consider how the models of the redesign of work will change these structures and flows.

The importance of tacit and explicit knowledge

Not all knowledge is the same. Some knowledge is *explicit* and objective – it's easy to write down and access and it moves with ease across your business. It's carried by manuals, websites and handbooks. In companies with a history of working virtually, much of the design of work is about making explicit as much knowledge as possible. That benefits new joiners and new team members, who can quickly get up to speed with how projects work and the skills of their colleagues.

Yet much of the valuable knowledge that resides within a company is *tacit* knowledge: the insights, know-how, mental models, ways of framing that are held in the minds of individuals and are part of how they see and interact with the world. Because this knowledge is held in the minds of individuals it is much more difficult than explicit knowledge to express and codify. Indeed, there is a view that you can only really access another's tacit knowledge when you know them and when you trust each other. So, whilst explicit knowledge stands outside of relationships codified in manuals and websites, tacit knowledge fundamentally resides within relationships. And if the nature, extent or depth of these relationships is changed by the redesign of work, then the fear is that this precious commodity will suffer.[1] So in the jobs that you are looking at, consider what knowledge is important to be productive in that job – how much is explicit in the sense that a new joiner could easily find this knowledge, and how much is implicit. If your proposed model of work will require more virtual working then you need to consider investing in more knowledge-capture processes to create more explicit knowledge.

Strong ties

Very early in the pandemic, by the spring of 2020 it became apparent that changing work patterns, and particularly working from home, was impacting on the development and maintenance of human connections and networks. We quickly learnt that many people were spending more of their time with people they already knew. Often these strengthening bonds turned out to be crucial to positive feelings of worth and mental health. In those tough situations people were taking solace from their nearest and dearest. Yet at the same time, people's relations with their broader network of colleagues, associates and more distant friends began to erode. Here are two comments I noted in my daily journal from managers in mid 2020 – when many had already experienced six months of lockdown.

'Some of the people in the team who are working from home are feeling very lonely. If they are naturally extroverts, this is really impacting on their happiness and well-being'; and, from another manager, 'At the moment, what really concerns me is the pressure on networks. People are getting close to each other and, frankly, that's been a lifesaver for many over the past months. But what has happened to the "water cooler" moments? It's impossible when everyone is at home to just accidentally bump into people.'

What is happening here is almost below the surface. Most of us don't systematically track our networks and few companies have empirical data on how knowledge flows within and across their business. Yet it is clear that if in your company the redesign of work includes changes to place and time, such as working from home or adopting a revised schedule, then this will inevitably impact on networks. For although often unobserved, networks will be significantly impacted by the redesign of work. That's why it is so important to understand how they work and how your redesign ideas will change them. In Figure 4 I illustrate some of the key concepts of this framework.[2]

The foundational concept is *ties* – the relationships that connect one person to another (each person in the network is shown as a node). These ties vary on a continuum from strong to weak.

Most of us have relatively few strong ties; these are with the people we know well, whom we trust and whom we can turn to for help and support. There is often a sense of balanced reciprocity in these relationships – people are happy to give to each other, but if one regularly takes more than they give, then over time the relationship will begin to deteriorate. Those you have strong ties with are people who know and understand you and who can empathize

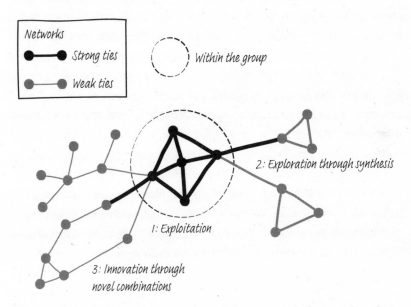

Figure 4. Framework: Human networks and the impact of strong and weak ties on the diffusion of knowledge.

with your situation (in the schema in Figure 4, these strong ties are shown by black lines). It turns out that with regard to the redesign of work, proximity is a significant driver of the formation of strong ties. Who you sit next to in the office and who you are likely to bump into in the corridor has a significant impact on how these strong ties are formed.

This powerful driver of proximity occurs throughout our lives. Take college friendships. There are potentially hundreds, possibly thousands of students with whom you could form lasting relationships. Yet, as those researchers who have tracked these relationships have discovered, the probability is that your closest and longest-lasting friendships will be formed with students rooming in adjacent dorms. In fact, in a series of studies researchers were able to compute a direct correlation between the degree of friendship and the dorm distance: the closer the dorm, the greater the probability of creating a long-lasting relationship.[3]

It's the power of proximity that is such an important factor in the design of offices. If, for example, all the marketing team sit closely together they get to know each other better, but they often fail to build relationships with other teams located in different floors – or even perhaps across the corridor. Using the power of proximity is crucial for the design group Arup, who have more than 15,000 specialists working in projects spanning 140 countries. As Arup principal Joe Correnza, who is based in the company's Melbourne office, told me:

> Bringing ideas from across all our disciplines is crucial for us. In the office we have engineers, designers, planners, technical specialists and consultants. We want them to talk with each other and bounce ideas off each other. One of the ways we do that is, within the office, to move teams from one place to another around every quarter.

These strong network ties can be important to *exploiting* the knowledge individual team members have (shown in the centre of the network framework). Because they know each other well and trust each other, they are more likely to share their tacit knowledge. Yet whilst these networks of strong ties are excellent at surfacing tacit knowledge – they are less able to create new ideas. Why? Because people are conversing about what they already know and their familiarity with each other's ideas means they are unlikely to encounter concepts that are new to them.

Weak ties

At the other end of the spectrum of relationships are weak ties (shown in the network schema as a grey line). These represent the links to the hundreds of people you are associated with. These are the acquaintances you meet less frequently and to whom you have little emotional attachment. You know something about them – for example, they would probably reply to an email you sent them – but you don't know much about their interests or family. You have many more of these weak ties precisely because they take less time and resources to maintain. Indeed, you may have many hundreds or even thousands of such connections on social media. Yet you probably devote less time to these large but weak networks than to maintaining your small number of strong ties.

The value of weak ties lies in their number: they have value precisely because there are so many of them. This was shown in one of the classic studies of networks carried out by Stanford sociologist Mark Granovetter, who studied the ways in which people found a new job.[4] (This research, by the way, preceded the growth of online job-search platforms such as LinkedIn and Monster, which have the potential to create thousands of potential job connections.) What he found was that when someone is looking for a new job, it is rarely a person they know well who originally suggests one. It is more likely to be a friend of a friend. Mark discovered that within groups of people who know each other very well there is much overlapping knowledge. So, if one of your close friends hears of a vacancy, it's likely that you'll also hear about it – because you have overlapping networks – and will pass that information on to another friend who is looking for a new job. It is through friends of friends – the power of weak ties – that new information is distributed, and it is here that serendipity often occurs.

In the network in Figure 4 you will notice that two members of the inner group have strong ties to members of other groups. These are boundary spanners: connecting two different networks together. When two distinct networks have very limited overlap in membership, it creates what sociologist Ron Burt terms a 'structural hole' in terms of the fields of knowledge.[5] A boundary spanner whose relationships connect both camps can bring together two completely different domains of knowledge – and the possibility of *exploration through synthesis*. Boundary spanners are in a position to explain the groups to each other, to point out areas of overlapping interest and to encourage people to question their basic paradigms and ways of working. As you think about the redesign of work it's worth considering who the boundary spanners might be in your own organization – does the redesign create natural channels for them to connect to others, or are you inadvertently blocking off these important channels?

Having many weak ties provides an exciting opportunity for a person to connect beyond their immediate group into the wider community. This is important because it offers an opportunity to be innovative and generate *innovation through novel combinations*.

The possible impact on these novel combinations was one of the greatest concerns for business during the pandemic. Many commentators talked about those 'water cooler' relationships. They began to realize that an office could be not only a place of close proximity but also a place where people made serendipitous encounters. There was a deeper anxiety that when people worked from home such encounters – and the creative sparks they set off – would be dramatically eroded. This is an important consideration as you redesign work. It highlights the importance of those precious times in the office both to create proximity and encourage serendipity.

The impact of technology on the creation of network ties

Before we leave our analysis of networks and knowledge flows it would be wise to factor in the impact of technology. There is no doubt that one of the distinguishing features of the pandemic was the speed that people adopted technologies such as Zoom and Microsoft Teams and the capacity of these technologies to deliver a low-cost/high-reliability service. We are beginning to realize that these technologies could play a crucial role in transforming how networks are formed and how knowledge flows.

In our strong network ties – with people we know well and trust – we naturally pivoted towards video meetings. But what of those relationships with people we didn't know so well – the weak ties? In Chapter 5 we will take a look at how companies like the Swedish technology group Ericsson are using online platforms to host conversations between many thousands of people over a period of three days. Might these virtual conversations be the base from which new networks are created – which could remain weak, but could also strengthen as people then catch up individually on video meetings?

Are these virtual connections the same as meeting people face to face, and are they likely to be the basis of serendipitous connections? Frankly, we don't know yet. Certainly, during lockdown, I made a couple of really good serendipitous connections with people I had not known previously. And after connecting with them over video conversations, I felt I had begun to know them relatively well.

Remember also that, looking forward, there is sure to be an avalanche of innovation around human connectivity. There is already much excitement about the possibilities of virtual and augmented reality in building and supporting networks. Take the accounting firm PwC, one of the major graduate recruiters in Europe. In the autumn of 2020 tens of thousands of fresh graduates joined the firm during lockdown. In previous years bringing them together face to face would have created wonderful opportunities for networks to be created – some of which would have been preserved for decades. But that year most of the new joiners never came near a PwC office. That might have been a disaster for these new joiners – but as Peter Brown, who heads PwC human resources for Europe, explained to me, the firm had made a few big technology investments that became game changers in the induction process. One of the most important was a virtual-reality platform. This created a virtual space where new joiners could move around a virtual conference venue, 'bumping' into each other, attending presentations by senior PwC people – even going on a virtual speedboat trip. In Peter's view the experience, though different from the normal induction, still worked. Feedback from graduates was as good, if not better than the norm. And as Peter and his colleagues went about redesigning work, the pandemic experience of using technology to create virtual networks began to shape their design thinking.

As you consider the current networks and knowledge flows in your business, bring a group together to discuss the points listed in Action #2.

Action #2
Understand how knowledge flows and how networks are structured

- Take the three job families you looked at in Action #1 and, using the networks framework shown in Figure 4 as a template, draft what you think were the pre-pandemic networks and knowledge flows that were central to those jobs. Were people primarily in tight network groups? Were there people who were boundary spanning to other groups? Did people have broad weak ties to many others both within and outside of the business?
- As you think about the current reality in your business consider how these networks and knowledge flows are currently operating. Has there been a shift in weak and

strong ties? If so, what impact might this have on the way that tacit knowledge flows and the possibility of new combinations of knowledge?

- Consider the impact of technologies such as video conferencing or virtual platforms on how these networks are formed and maintained. In what way are they substituting for face-to-face connections? What are the potential challenges, and also the benefits?

Understand: What people want from work and from the company

My doctoral thesis was on Maslow's hierarchy of needs. I was fascinated by how our background and experience shape what we need and desire.[6] That research was an early lesson in realizing that people are not all the same, and at various points in their lives their needs and desires change. From the perspective of redesigning work, it makes sense to start by looking at the people in your company. It is likely there are groups of people with relatively similar needs and desires. The data from employee surveys or focus groups will give you a sense of what these are. Their needs will be the result of a whole host of factors – a person's current life-cycle stage, age, background, experience, personality and so on. Whilst the results of employee surveys can be useful, my preference is to bring energy to these data by building a number of *personas* that create a compelling narrative of what it 'feels' like to be this person. (We will take a look at two of these in a moment.)

Yet whilst you can look at what people need *now*, it's also possible to imagine what they might need and aspire to in the *future*. That's important because in redesigning work, the aim is to create a way of working that has validity and benefits both now *and* in the future. And to do that you need to have a perspective on the broad, universal trends that will over the coming years shape what people want from work. And, moreover, to really think about what all this means for 'the deal' between the organization and the individual.

What people want now – creating personas helps the insight process

People are different and have a range of needs, wants and ways of working. One way of simplifying this is to use the concept of a persona. A persona is a fictional account of an individual that captures one or more aspects of their demography, their situation, their needs and aspirations. It is in a sense a pictorial representation of the survey data. As a teacher, I create personas to help my students think through tough issues. For example, when we look at the issues of an ageing workforce I have three personas of people of different ages – twenty-five, forty and sixty-five. I ask the students to consider what each persona would want from work and how an organization can support them. Almost inevitably, the class (of twenty- and thirty-somethings) looking at the persona of the sixty-five-year-old struggle to think about how the company can support them. By getting 'under the skin', as it were, of this persona the students can empathize more profoundly with their older subjects' situation.

The advantage of personas is that our brain typically finds narratives and stories easier to make sense of than statistics and data. Thinking through a persona – let's call him Roger – who is sixty-five and worried about his pension, is easier than being presented with pages of data about the demography of sixty-five-year-olds, their aspirations, savings rate, health outcomes and so on.

When you create four or five personas you give your colleagues a sense of what it feels like to work in these job families as each persona captures a number of aspects of the work and employee data. I've found it useful to present these personas to managers and ask what these new ways of working would mean for these personas. Managers can then discuss with their peers and hear how others would approach these personas. As you will see in Action

#3, I suggest that, as part of this design step, you create a number of personas to act as a narrative structure to your debates about the redesign of work.

As an exercise in thinking through the impact of homeworking, I created two personas I called Julio and Mandy, both of whom work as strategic planners in a Chicago-based multinational, and both of whom worked from home during the lockdown.

Julio is loving life. He lives in a large house in the suburbs of Chicago with his teenager kids. Before the pandemic he'd spent long hours in the office and this, plus a ninety-minute commute each way, meant he was rarely home before 9 p.m. after leaving at 6.30 a.m. We can imagine Julio basking in the sheer pleasure of getting up later, walking the dogs in the day, spending time with his kids. He feels healthier than he has for years. And whilst he misses the comradery of his colleagues in the office, he's been at this firm for over a decade: so, to use the network terms, he already has strong ties with his team and numerous weak ties with people across the business. As he reflects on his experience, he feels he is fitter, less stressed and possibly even more productive. Certainly, he does not feel his productivity has diminished. As Julio thinks about how he wants to work in the next few years, he is keen to continue to work from home – at least some of the time. In fact, he's talked to his partner about this and they are of the view that if he's not given the option to work from home he will look for another organization where this is possible – even if that means taking a salary cut.

One of Julio's colleagues is Mandy. She's in her late twenties and has been in the company for one year fresh out of an MBA programme. When she moved to Chicago she rented an apartment with three bedrooms and small communal space which she shared with two roommates. During 2018 and 2019 that worked perfectly. All her co-renters worked the same long hours as her, so they barely met each other except during their communal Sunday brunches. She'd chosen the apartment to be as near as possible to the office, just a fifteen-minute walk away, and she could pop into the gym before work and easily meet friends for drinks later. Looking back, her lockdown experience has been very different from Julio's. Within weeks, tensions began to build in the apartment as all three flatmates tried to work from home using a single internet connection which was under particular strain from one flatmate, nicknamed the 'data whale', who routinely downloaded huge visual projects for the PR agency she worked at. And to make matters worse, within a month of the start of the pandemic, one of her sharers had lost her job. Her anxiety was upsetting them all.

So, by April 2020, Mandy was working out of her tiny bedroom on a makeshift desk sitting on a dining chair. And she was missing terribly the casual camaraderie of the office – catching up with people, listening to stories, drinking coffee . . .

But there was more that was worrying her. As a new joiner she had relished going into the office to meet her workmates. She'd particularly enjoyed watching Julio interact with his colleagues about the strategy of the business. She'd learnt a lot from the new data he brought to their attention and then the way he used this as a basis to begin to change the way others looked at the strategic challenges they faced. To coin the famous phrase from the musical *Hamilton* – she relished 'being in the room where it happened'. Mandy is in an 'observation' phase of her professional development: she's hypersensitive to cues, listening hard for changes in tone, watching carefully how people interact. She is beginning to create an idea of what the business is really about.

Mandy may be a fictional persona, but her situation is replicated around the major cities of the world. That's why, when you think about the challenges of redesigning work, it is young people like Mandy who have to be considered. If in the redesign of work the company decides that the strategy planning group will work primarily from home, what will this mean for Mandy's day-to-day experience? For her, like Julio, the redesign of work will be a key factor in her decision whether to stay or join another company. Right now, whilst she's happy to work from home occasionally, her plan is to be office-based.

It's the accumulation of the individual stories of people like Julio and Mandy that will be crucial to a successful redesign of work. It is their hopes and aspirations that begin to paint a picture of what people want. Of course, what this immediately shows is that people – even in the same job – may prefer different ways of working. And, as we will see in the next chapter, that puts a significant emphasis on designing work that both acknowledges their individual needs whilst also emphasizing the organization's need to create a culture of high performance.

You can understand the needs of individual employees by listening to them and surveying their preferences. You can also bring them together in large virtual conversations to talk about how they see the development of work using a process of co-creation, which we will look at in Chapter 5.

What will people want in the future?

Within your company and among your employees there will be a range of individual personal characteristics and situations that will impact on what people want from work. So it's important you listen to and acknowledge these individual differences. Yet it's also important that you design for the future, and to do that you need to take a broader lens and consider the wider universal trends that will accelerate in the coming years and will shape what people want and need. These trends relate to longevity, society and automation. They will inevitably shape what people want now and – importantly – are likely to want in the future.

TO STAY HEALTHY

As people make choices about where they work and how they work, one of the big factors they will take into consideration is whether working for your company will help them stay healthy. They are more likely to join your business if they see that they can be healthy and are more likely to leave if they believe working for your company is having an adverse impact on their health.

Think of it this way – at the very beginning of the industrializa-
tion of work in the 1850s the average length of life was forty-five.
Granted, that is the mean figure skewed by the fact that a significant proportion of the population died as infants, but the point is
this – when life was short, then thirty years of working life was the
span many people could anticipate. Now, looking forward, it is not
beyond the bounds of possibility that you, your children and colleagues will live one hundred years.

It's perhaps no surprise that many people who read *The 100-Year
Life*, the book I wrote with the economist Andrew Scott, were aston-
ished by the enormous strides that were being made in longevity. In
general, life expectancy is increasing in many countries of the world
by two years every decade. That's the result of a combination of
healthier living and medical interventions (particularly tackling the
diseases of middle age such as heart failure). The bottom line is that
living to a hundred is in the grasp of our children, perhaps even you.
This is sure to have a profound impact on what people want from
work at your company.

One major impact is on financing. If your employees live longer,
they will want (and need) to work longer. Here is the simple
truth – unless you've saved around 15 per cent of your income
from the first day you started working, you are unlikely to have
accumulated sufficient resources to retire at sixty-five. And it's
increasingly unlikely that you can look to government funds to provide any meaningful support for those decades. So, the reality, and
it's a reality that is dawning on many people, is that being gainfully
employed through their seventies and possibly longer is going to be
a priority.

This new rhythm and cadence will inevitably shape people's aspirations for work. If you believe you've a chance to live into your
nineties or beyond then you care a great deal more about being
healthy. No one wants to live to ninety and experience ten or twenty
years of ill health. We want to stride into our eighties fit and healthy.
To do that, people need to build and maintain healthy living and
working practices from the start of their adult lives. What might

these healthy living practices be? I've quizzed those who run longevity centres about what they personally do to live a healthy long life. Their responses are remarkably similar – take exercise every day, eat healthy foods, sleep eight hours a night. Simple as that. And those who are especially interested in living a happy long life told me to give time to friends and family and to the community.

What does this mean for redesigning work? Faced with several options for how and when to work, many people will choose work that enables them to stay healthy. This means having sufficient autonomy over time schedules that enable them to sleep eight hours a night; it means having predictable working hours so they can make plans to walk with others, meet family and friends and not have to constantly cancel their social appointments.

TO HAVE A BALANCED FAMILY LIFE

As work evolves to encompass the public space (the office) and the private space (the home), so relationships and families become more central to the choices people make about work. And when they are making these decisions, they are likely to be taking into consideration the needs of another working person.

It is fascinating to watch the speed at which family structures are changing.[7] In most countries, women now work. That is a stark contrast to the home lives of people like me, born in the 1950s with a mother who was a home carer and a father who worked. This had changed by the 1970s, when a majority of women began to enter the workplace. In general they were more educated than their mothers and likely to have aids such as washing machines and freezers which significantly reduced the hours spent in domestic labour. Yet in this first wave, working women often moved into part-time roles once they became mothers. And even if they returned to full-time work, their income was likely to go down and in fact rarely caught up with their male counterparts. That inevitably reinforced the norms in the house that it was the man's work and the demands of his job that took priority.

These norms began to change as more women built careers and – for a number of reasons, including legislation – received similar wages to men. Moreover, because these women had their children later (mid thirties rather than mid twenties) and had fewer of them (two rather than four) they were building career paths that were equivalent in speed and remuneration to men. Over time, couples moved from 'male career/female carer' to 'male career/female job' to 'male career/female career' or 'male carer/female career'. In fact, by 2019 the 'dual career' was a social phenomenon that was described in books and articles and debated widely.[8]

At the same time, family structures morphed into a broader variety: single mothers and single fathers brought up their kids independently; men had a child through a surrogate; women used a sperm donor to conceive; people in their fifties divorced and some remarried, creating elongated families with an array of step-children; with five generations alive, some families had grandparents in the household; some people were spending a significant chunk of their adult life as a single person.

What does this mean for the redesign of work? It's important you don't make assumptions about an employee's personal life: fathers might be just as interested in childcare and parental leave as mothers, and not every adult has or wants children. One global professional company, for instance, found that over 60 per cent of its employees were single and either living on their own or with a parent or partner. This has implications for bringing issues of inclusion and diversity to the fore to ensure that the norms and practices of work are fair and just, whatever an individual's personal circumstances.

TO LEARN (FASTER THAN MACHINES)

One of the results of working from home during the pandemic was to accelerate a trend that was already in play – the automation of work and the digitalization of processes such as learning and scheduling. Looking forward, the impact of technology on work continues to be profound and for the majority of employees the reality is that part of their job (in some cases a significant part) will be automated. That's both a huge source of anxiety – will I lose my job or be downgraded to a lower paid position? – and a source of motivation – I need to reskill or upskill to stay relevant.

It's no surprise that as you look to redesigning work it is technology that will create many of the options you will be considering. It could be that, like PwC in their induction of joiners, you explore using virtual and augmented reality to try to recreate the magic of serendipitous connections. You might be using scheduling programs to reduce the potential nightmare of endless meetings. And tools like data analytics to coordinate when and where teams work and create performance feedback loops.

All of these changing work habits are sure to speed up the automation of work. The experience of the pandemic has encouraged some companies to make big bets on automation investments as they have discovered that customers have become more willing to interact with a chatbot – particularly if the service is smooth and efficient. And as employees moved from the office to home their employers discovered that in many cases productivity held up.

Of course the automation of work and replacement of tasks by robots and artificial intelligence (AI) is not a new story. As early as 2015 economists predicted the wholesale transformation of jobs, as many tasks could be performed at lower cost and more predictably by a machine. Jobs like cab driving would transform as autonomous vehicles reached the roads, and jobs like accountancy would morph as AI-enabled programs replaced more routine tasks. In fact, it's been calculated that for most people, 60 per cent of the tasks that make up their job can and will be automated.[9]

To some executives, including Facebook's CEO Mark Zuckerberg, the capacity to use virtual connectivity has opened up the opportunity to hire key workers such as engineers far from Facebook's main offices. That is sure to uncover new pools of talent in areas that had not traditionally been seen as talent pools. Other CEOs asked the same question: if a job could now be done virtually in a high-cost city, couldn't it be performed in the home of someone in a lower-cost city – with a lower wage package? That echoes the switch from high-cost to low-cost countries that was made in the 1990s in call-centre work as companies offshored or outsourced this type of work. It is possible that knowledge-based work will follow the same trend and this is sure to put ever more pressure on workers in high-cost countries to upskill to higher-value work.

What does this mean for the redesign of work? As you begin to consider what this pathway of automation will mean for your employees it's worth understanding that, as people get a sense of how their job might change, they will put more emphasis on work and organizations that enable them to *upskill* as part of their current job. And for those who believe their job will significantly change, they will be looking to the organization to support them to *reskill* and move to a completely different job. So, as people understand the extent to which automation will transform their work, they will be particularly interested in the capacity of the business to support them to learn, to navigate their careers and to certify their skills.

TO LIVE A MULTISTAGE LIFE

Even before the pandemic, many employees were facing two major shocks to their working-life plans: the possibility that they will live longer, and therefore work for longer; and the likelihood that profound technological innovations will continuously replace and augment the tasks they are skilled in. Together, these are sure to impact on what they want from work and the trade-offs they are willing to accept.

In my own research I have seen how these shocks impact people's attitudes to the stages of their life. Many are realizing that the typical 'three-stage' life of full-time education, full-time work and full-time retirement is poorly aligned to the needs of longer lives with constant upskilling and reskilling.

What is emerging is what my colleague Andrew Scott and I have called the 'multistage life'.[10] We could see how the education stage is extending into lifelong learning as those in their forties go back to college, or those in their sixties register for online learning courses. The traditional stage of full-time work is fragmenting as people are taking time out of their working lives to care for their children or ageing parents, start their own side-hustle business or travel and explore. We could also see changes occurring in the final, retirement stage of life. It is as if people are reallocating this time. The 'leisure' time of traditional end-of-life retirement is being chunked into months or years and introduced into what was the working stage of life as people take sabbaticals or time off to travel and learn.

Every generation is facing up to this new reality in its own way. Many in their forties and fifties are already planning how best to make a switch that will ensure they continue to develop their capabilities. People currently in their sixties are taking a step back to reflect on what might be thirty or forty years that lie ahead of them. Some are embracing this as an extraordinary gift and rethinking how they want to spend their lives in ways that they had not previously imagined. Others are wondering what they can do now to ensure they bridge the gap.

We can also expect, as the lifetime sequence of work becomes more free-flowing, that more life stages will naturally emerge. Some people will take time out across their whole life to explore their options. This was a choice that once only younger people took in their 'gap year'; it's now seen as a viable option whatever someone's age. Some will want to become an independent producer, even perhaps an entrepreneur, creating the opportunity at any age to build resources independent of a company. This shift is reflected in the Kauffman Index of Entrepreneurial Activity: the number of entrepreneurs aged between fifty-five and sixty-four rose every year from around 18 per cent in 1996, to over 25 per cent in 2018.[11] And more people are actively creating a 'portfolio' life in which activities focused on making money are balanced with activities that are more community focused.

As you gain a deeper understanding of how longevity will transform what your employees need and want, it will be no longer appropriate to assume that 'age equals stage' – that from knowing an employee's age it is possible to predict their life stage and there-fore their likely needs and aspirations. You will have to take a more personalized approach to understanding your employees. For example, an employee could be twenty-five and want to take time out to explore – but that could also be true of someone who is forty-five or sixty-five. And again, an employee could be sixty and want to build a portfolio life but others could be aspiring to do this at thirty or fifty. As life paths become more free-flowing, flexibility will be a real benefit for those employees who are moving away from the traditional three-stage life. These employees will truly value the opportunity to take a sabbatical, live in another country, job-share or work part time to build a business on the side.

How much flexibility will talented people be prepared to give up?

These broader, universal trends (longevity, society, automation) and an acknowledgement of a multistage life will inevitably shape what it is that employees want and need at various times in their working lives. As you reflect on these for your own company you will want to consider the alignment between what people want and what the organization needs.

These issues play out in significant ways in terms of what it is you want your employees to do, and what they want from work at that point in time. Realizing this and designing work around this 'deal' will be crucial – but it's not straightforward – particularly when it comes to flexibility. To illustrate some of the issues this raises take a look at the framework in Figure 5.

Imagine you are an executive in an investment company – take Goldman Sachs or one of the prestigious law firms. As you seek to understand the needs of your current and future employees it's likely that two variables are uppermost in your mind. First, you want people who are at the highest level of potential and talent to join you and then stay. That's the promise to your clients, who expect to be interacting with highly talented people, and it's the promise to team leaders, who expect to have highly talented colleagues.

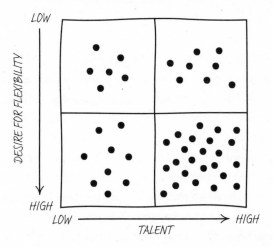

Figure 5. Framework: Talent and the desire for flexibility.

However, it's likely there is another variable that you will prioritize, and that's people's needs and expectations for flexible ways of working. And specifically, you probably want to attract and retain people who do *not* prioritize flexibility. It is those people in the top-right quadrant of Figure 5 who interest you. These are people who are prepared to work in an office, so will accept limited flexibility about place. You might recall David Solomon, the chairman of Goldman Sachs, commenting in the spring of 2021 that working from home was 'an aberration'. He was keen that, as soon as possible, employees would return to work in the office. He was not alone. Andrew Monk, chief executive of investment bank VSA Capital, told BBC Radio 5 Live:

> In the financial services industry it can be a problem if people work from home. People working from home don't realize it, but they're gradually getting slower and slower whereas the people in the office aren't. In the financial services industry you need to discuss ideas and discuss what's going on. People working from home miss out on an awful lot of the activity in the office because we don't have time to tell them.

You are also likely to want people who do not prioritize flexibility around time. In order to serve client needs there is an expectation of availability for a great deal of the time – be that evenings, weekends, or holidays. You want people to work closely with clients, often on significant deals under intense pressure, and to cooperate by pulling knowledge and insight from across teams and networks at speed.

So if your ideal potential and current employees are not prioritizing flexibility of time and place, what are they prioritizing? On the face of it, the obvious priority is income. At this point in time (and possibly for the future) the thing people in these roles most want is a high income. That is why, for example, Goldman Sachs, like other investment banks, increased the offer to new graduate associate joiners in the summer of 2021 to $110,000 per annum in what some newspapers at the time called 'a war for talent'. The major law firms (also recruiting from the top-right quadrant) did the same by raising the entry-level pay of young lawyers to $200,000.

Yet these joiners are likely to have other priorities beyond money. When people join these firms they know that by doing so they are sending a signal to their current network and future employers they are now part of an elite group. Think of it as a play in reputation boosting.

They are also likely to be learning a great deal from their colleagues and clients. This was clear in a study of companies like Goldman Sachs conducted by Harvard Business School professor Boris Groysberg.[12] He asked a simple question: when people leave hothouse companies like Goldman Sachs to go to other firms, does their performance decrease, remain the same, or increase? To answer this question he analysed the performance data of analysts before and after they entered a new company. He discovered that when people leave a company (often for competitors) their performance decreases. Why might this be so? Looking more deeply at this he discovered that, as expected, part of what propelled these new joiners to be successful was their own talent. But crucially, a significant part of their success had been created by the networks they had formed within their previous company. They had been used to reaching out to trusted colleagues for the insight about a particular company or CEO, or meeting their team to brainstorm what might happen in a particular merger, or asking people in their networks to broker an introduction. Shorn of these relationships and networks, their performance and ultimately their productivity suffered until they could create new networks.

So, if you are recruiting in the top-right quadrant (high talent/low flexibility) then you may need to assume that, with regard to your understanding of these people, they prioritize and want three things: a high income, a reputational boost and projects and colleagues they can learn from.

On the other hand, maybe you're hoping to recruit from the same talent pool as Goldman Sachs and the elite law firms, but you want to go after those highly talented people in the bottom-right quadrant – those who are talented but also prioritize flexibility.

Dario Kosarac heads up CPP Investments, a global investment management organization that invests the assets of the Canadian Pension Plan. He told me that when he is thinking about talent for the firm he looks to the long term and what will keep them on board. 'We are pursuing the "golden model",' he said. 'We don't want to be a place that exploits and burns people out. We want to keep our colleagues engaged, motivated and balanced.' There's still attrition, but, he says, 'we aim to retain most colleagues over the long term'. As I'll explain later in the book, this plays out in a host of flexibility options including sabbaticals and a recently launched 'work from anywhere for three months' practice.

Similarly, it was this pool of talent within this high-talent/high-flexibility quadrant that Christy Johnson, who founded the strategy consulting practice Artemis Connection, was most fascinated by. Fresh out of Stanford and working with the consulting firm

McKinsey, Christy realized that she needed a more flexible way of working – and she was not alone. As she told my MBA class in the spring of 2021:

> I was obsessed by a report the McKinsey research institute had published about talent.[13] Even in 2015 with a tight labour market, they calculated that the productivity loss of underemployed talent in the US ran at $1.7 billion. They described caregivers or amazingly talented people living in non-urban centres. They cited a US survey that three-quarters of stay-at-home mothers would be likely to work if they had flexible options.[14] When I founded Artemis in 2015, this was the group I wanted to tap into.

This meant for Christy intentionally designing work that enabled people to work from home and to work flexible hours.

It's possible that, like Dario and Christy, you will be operating in very tight labour markets, perhaps with job skills that are hard to find and retain. That puts a real premium on understanding what people want – both now and in the future – and how they are prioritizing their needs.

Action #3
Understand what people want

- Take a closer look at the job families you identified in Action #1 and consider the type of people who do these jobs. What do you know about their personal circumstances? What do they care about and aspire to? What motivates them?
- Sketch out four personas which best represent your typical employees. For each persona describe the job they do, their name, age, gender and personal circumstances. These personas will be used in later actions.
- Consider the four major trends I have described: longevity/health, society/family, automation/learning and

multistage lives. Are these trends you have seen in your employee population and, if so, what specific aspects are more salient?

- How are people prioritizing their needs – what's the deal that will attract the sort of people you need?

Understand: The experience of work

Who we are – our age, stage of life, gender, personal experiences – all impact on what we want from work now and in the future. That is why understanding this is foundational to the redesign of work.

Yet as you think about understanding and empathizing with employees, it's important to go beyond these broad trends and ask, 'How are people actually experiencing work?' Knowing how they are experiencing work can act as a platform from which you can analyse the likely future impact of the redesign of work.

I'm intrigued by how we think about employees' experiences of work, and in my Future of Work Consortium the team at my advisory company HSM Advisory made this a research theme in June 2021. Over a period of six months we interviewed executives about their experiences and then ran a two-day virtual masterclass which brought together more than seventy-four executives from eighteen of our partner companies whom we engaged with in a series of co-creation experiences. Our aim was to come to a shared view of how to be sure that the redesign of work would be a positive experience for employees.

It's easy as you go about redesigning work to focus too much on the job and the tasks without really asking what work means to people: what is memorable about work? Of course, each of us, and each of our colleagues, have our own personal experience of work, but beyond that there are collective experiences that we share and that will fundamentally impact on how we experience the redesign of work. To get a sense of this I asked those seventy-four executives to tell me their most memorable experience of work. Here are some of these responses – shown in the word cloud opposite.

Perhaps these recollections resonated with some of your own memories of work. These recollections are important because they make a real difference to how we feel about work and shape our engagement and likelihood of staying and being productive. And as we set about redesigning work, it's important to understand what these events are and how they are likely to be impacted by changes in work.

Looking more closely at the word cloud you will see the experiences of work typically fall into one of three categories. Some are *painful* and have negative emotions associated with them. Things like *getting the sack, being pulled off a project* or *a brutal conversation with my boss*. So, as people look to the redesign of work, one of the questions they will be asking themselves is, 'Will this experience cause me pain, or will it reduce the possibility of pain?' Some of these experiences are, in a sense, a *gain*; we feel positive when they happen – *getting promoted, getting a qualification, hosting my first town-hall meeting, travelling to the US*. A question people will ask themselves of the redesign of work is, 'Will this help me maximize what I gain, or will it take this away from me?' There are some memories of work that are specific to that person and their *needs* at that time. Take a look at the word cloud and you will see some of these – *telling my boss I was pregnant, empathy during a time I was ill*. So, as people think about the redesign of work they will be asking, 'Does this meet my current needs and expectations?' And naturally, these needs and expectations change over the course of our working life and indeed in the face of specific experiences such as having a child.

Take another look at the comments opposite in light of your ideas about redesigning work. For example, if you decide to move to virtual working, which of these events would be most impacted and is this likely to increase the pain or improve the gain?

Starting in a new team.

Getting promoted.

My first day in Japan.

The first Christmas party.

Telling my boss
I was pregnant.

Being pulled off
a project.

Getting the sack.

Leading a conference.

The last day at the company.

Getting a qualification.

A brutal
conversation
with my boss.

Empathy during a
time I was ill.

Hosting my first
town-hall meeting.

Starting in a
new company.

Travelling to the US.

Winning a new piece
of work.

First day in our new office.

The digitalization of experiences

How we think about work and our expectations of working are influenced by our own experiences – our life stage or life events. They are also influenced by our specific experiences of our life outside of work – how we buy, how we spend our leisure time, what we learn and how we learn. Inevitably for many people these out-of-work experiences were changed by the pandemic.

Think of it this way – when you sit down in the evenings to watch Netflix or another streaming platform you are experiencing a highly *personalized* service based on recommendations from your profile's unique watch history. This inevitably shapes your expectations of personalization. Next morning as you start to work it's likely you judge your work experience against the same expectations of personalization. And if during the day you use a financial platform like Monzo, you experience services that seem to *intuitively* match how you live. You wonder whether the tools you use at work have that same level of intuition. And you are likely to be becoming ever more used to *frictionless* experiences. When you order a meal through an app like Deliveroo your options are presented in one place – you don't need to call multiple restaurants to find out what is available and then agree the delivery times.

Our experience of digital technologies, which were accelerated during the pandemic, have shaped our and our employees' expectations. So when we think about the redesign of work we expect to have experiences that are as personalized as Netflix, as intuitive as Monzo and as frictionless as Deliveroo. Let's take a look now at how you can understand these employee experiences and then later circle back to consider how they can be factored into models of work.

Insight: How HSBC understood employees' experiences

In creating ways to understand employees' experiences, there is much we can learn from how the marketing discipline analyses and understands consumer experiences.

Leanne Cutts was the Chief Marketing Officer (CMO) at the global bank HSBC and in this role was supported by my advisory group HSM Advisory in a series of large-scale conversations that took place across the bank. She described to me how she has found three tools useful to understand the employee experience: the customer journey model, a new employee journey model and the Net Promoter Score (NPS) tool.

The HSBC marketing team had been building insight into customer experiences for decades, and to create the same depth of employee insight Leanne built a multidisciplinary team of people from business strategy, communications, human resources and marketing. They used design thinking and data analytics to understand employee experience. As she told me, 'We have a real opportunity to tap into the rich sources of information about our 230,000 employees.'

The team began by mapping the employee journey from the point of recruitment, through onboarding and performance and then the final stage of the journey, when they separate from the firm and take the memories of their working experience into their family, networks and community. The experience of the pandemic inevitably changed the onboarding experience whilst also bringing into the frame working from home and hybrid work. As Leanne commented, 'We had been trying to encourage our employees and consumers to use digital channels. With the experience of the pandemic this has become a flood – people now see digital as non-negotiable for a much wider range of activities.'

By mapping the experiences of specific groups, the design team got a sense of how any redesign model would impact them. Take, for example, the graduate journey. Using both quantitative and qualitative data, the team were able to understand, from the graduate's perspective, both the pains and the gains. It turns out that one of the most significant points of a graduate's experience is the transition from one six-month placement to another. When this goes well, it's a significant gain to the graduate as they move into their next role feeling positive and confident. However, when it's done badly, it can be a painful experience, often leaving the graduate struggling to see how they can contribute or understand what is expected of them.

So, as the HSBC team went about redesigning work, they focused on this transition, realizing, for example, that because line managers were so important in these crucial transitional points, a checklist would need to be developed to steer their behaviours. The team also mapped the employee journey in detail, taking a closer look at exactly what the graduates were learning – from both the formal training programmes and their mentors and team leaders. This mapping exercise made clear the growing gap between the digital and data skill needs of the bank and the extent to which graduates were learning these skills. As a consequence, the bank introduced streams of personalized learning activity focused on building digital and data skills.

As Leanne reflected on how HSBC had learnt to understand the employee experience of work she pointed to their use of the Net Promoter Score:

> It has been highly transformative with customers and helped us to identify and then solve specific problems. So we decided to pilot an Employee Net Promoter Score to identify the particular circumstances that are creating pain and gain. It rapidly became part of a regular feedback loop with managers and was crucial in reducing frustrations about work because we listen and solve the challenges more quickly.

I talked to Leanne and other executives about what they had learnt from their insight into customer experience that had implications for employee experience and the redesign of work. They made two points. First, in redesigning work it's crucial to simplify and reduce complexity by harmonizing the various processes. As one executive commented about the employee experience, 'We had too many systems and it was hard for people to make sense of them. So, when we introduce a new platform now we make sure it's compatible and can be embedded in our existing systems.' They did this by using a crowdsourcing platform to ask people which processes stopped them from getting things done fast. The significant pain points they identified were around performance management, and the team then focused on how best to simplify this.

They also drew attention to what they'd learnt from customer experiences about using technology wisely. In order to humanize the design of the employee experience that means, for example, matching the employee experience to the degree of human–machine interface. So when the experience is highly personal, such as a bereavement, it's a human-to-human connection that builds a sense of empathy and belonging. However, if it's a shared routine experience such as mandatory training, then human-to-machine enables the process to be quicker and more streamlined. That was the conclusion of the IBM team who developed the chatbot Myca, which matches employees with internal vacancies, learning opportunities or adjacent career paths. And for something such as onboarding, which is both a shared and an individual experience, then a combination of human-to-machine-to-human both delivers a shared, high-quality experience whilst also reinforcing the importance of human connections.

Action #4
Understand the experience of work

- Take a closer look at the key experiences that people have working for your company. What are the experiences that are likely to cause pain? Which are experiences of gain?

Are these experiences meeting employees' needs and expectations?

- Find out about the employee journey – from the point they are considering joining the organization to the point they leave it. What is this telling you about employees' experiences? It might be worthwhile to follow Leanne Cutts of HSBC and put together a multidisciplinary team from marketing, human resources, communications and strategy to work on this.

- Consider experimenting with marketing tools such as Net Promoter Score and repurposing them to focus on employees. That will give you a sense of the events that are creating pain or gain. As you begin to redesign work, are there ways you can redesign those events that currently cause pain, and are there ways of accentuating those that create gain?

3. *Reimagine*

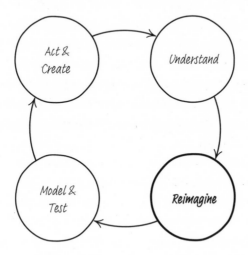

This is an exciting phase of the redesign of work. You now understand what drives productivity in some of the key jobs in the business – whether that be energy, focus, coordination or cooperation. You've learnt something about how networks are structured within teams and across the business and how this is likely to impact on the flow of both tacit and explicit knowledge. You've understood what employees want and need – whether it's their individual profile or more general long-term aspirations around staying healthy, creating stable happy relationships, learning faster than machines or creating a multistage life plan. And you have taken a closer look at the experience of being an employee in your business.

It's now time to reimagine work. In this chapter I'll share with you ways of thinking about design choices around both place and time. These are not straightforward options. Almost any choice you make about place and time will have real benefits, but also potentially significant downsides and trade-offs. So before you jump into modelling and testing your new work design, it's wise to think through how best to increase these benefits whilst also acknowledging and confronting the trade-offs.

We begin by looking at place – both co-located (typically office working) and distributed (usually homeworking). I share what companies are doing to ensure that the office – be that a shared office, a satellite or a hub – truly becomes a place of real cooperation where innovation can flourish. I then show how working from home, though a potential source of energy, needs significant effort in boundary management to reach these optimum working outcomes.

Then we look at time – both synchronous (when people are connected) and asynchronous (when people are disconnected from others). Synchronous time can be a real boost for coordination, but this requires intentional work scheduling including intermittent connectivity and working rituals to really deliver performance. And for asynchronous time to support productive focused work, there needs again to be intentional work design around establishing blocks of time.

Here are the five aspects we will be taking a closer look at, with a number of frameworks as thought starters for you and your colleagues, followed by the action steps to engage with.

Reimagine: Place and time
- Framework: Place and asynchronous/synchronous time
- Frameworks: The potential choice and impact of place/ time and productivity
- Action #5

Reimagine place: The office as a place of cooperation
- Framework: Productivity elements and office types
- Insight: Fujitsu and Arup
- Action #6

Reimagine place: The home as a source of energy
   – Framework: Boundary management
   – Insight: BT and TCS
   – Action #7
Reimagine time: Asynchronous time as an opportunity for
   focus
   – Framework: Focus – humans and machines
   – Action #8
Reimagine time: Synchronous time as a driver of
   coordination
   – Insight: TCS and Telstra
   – Action #9

Reimagine: Place and time

The pandemic created an opportunity to rethink work in terms of both place and time, and in doing so created a whole host of opportunities and challenges: What is the optimal level of flexibility around where and when people do their jobs? Should you move towards being more virtual, as the team at Artemis Connection have done, or bring everyone into the office, as Goldman Sachs is doing, or, like CPP Investments, build a whole portfolio of flexible working practices around place? As you look around you can see that some leaders are reimagining work happening 'anywhere', others are asking employees to return to central office spaces, some are accommodating flexible time commitments, others are requiring staff to be available at core times such as nine to five.

Who's right? As I've shown, the type of jobs, networks and people tend to differ across companies. And faced with this variety it's clear that when you think about your own company you need to develop what is right for you – your own signature. There is no one-size-fits-all solution, no silver bullet, no list of best practices to copy. Rather, it is the design process that began in Chapter 2 with understanding that will become the basic canvas from you to reimagine work.

Reframing place and time

You can begin to imagine place and time by taking a closer look at the framework I've presented in Figure 6.

PLACE (CO-LOCATED / DISTRIBUTED)

Perhaps you have already experimented and redesigned work around place by establishing homeworking, or creating hubs where people have the opportunity to work closer to home. The companies who have done this have already learnt a great deal about how these new ways of working actually play out in practice. However, it's important to realize that in most of these pioneering companies these experiments with homeworking took place in environments such as call centres. These are usually jobs with much explicit knowledge and where coordination is not crucial – typically people who work in call centres are relatively independent, spending limited time coordinating with each other.

Before early 2020 it was relatively unusual for corporate-based knowledge workers to work from home. For this type of work, the place of productivity was the office. Separate from personal space and outfitted with all the furniture and technology necessary to do jobs efficiently, the office was a place of congregation, where

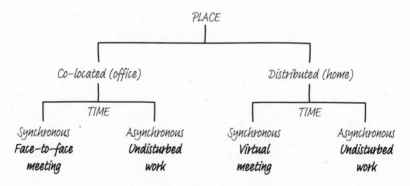

Figure 6. Framework: The choices of place and time.

people gathered for one primary goal – to work. The impact of the pandemic was to dramatically move the design of work. For some, their place of work is now located in their personal space – their home.

TIME (SYNCHRONOUS/ASYNCHRONOUS)

Before the pandemic, the majority of knowledge workers in their everyday tasks synchronized their time with others – they worked the same hours as their colleagues, often punctuated by many face-to-face meetings. Perhaps you had already experimented with time – adopting a four-day week, compressing time schedules, introducing part-time work. Yet in general these experiments with time took place in specific industries or in the case of part-time work were primarily associated with professions such as nursing, teaching or retail. And in those jobs the general view was that working part-time was an impediment to long-term career success.

The impact of the pandemic was to change the way we imagined time. As many people started to work from home they had a chance to be imaginative about how they spent the time they had clawed back from commuting. But it worked both ways as work schedules extended into 'private' time and work was fitted into personal schedules – caring for family and friends, taking time out to keep healthy and fit, even doing professional upskilling. And as the control of time shifted, there was a growing awareness of the nature of time and synchronizing with others. For some tasks it was becoming clear that *asynchronous* work – disconnected from others – was possible and perhaps even preferable. And there was a growing awareness that, at a period when many tasks were distributed and carried out away from the office, being *synchronized* and working at the same time as others could have real benefits.

Looking back to Figure 3, when we considered the productive elements, one of the crucial questions is how to create a context of work (both place and time) that best enables the productive elements (energy, focus, coordination, cooperation) that are critical to the key jobs in your company.

I think about this as a series of frameworks I have illustrated in Figures 7 and 8. Figure 7 shows the whole range of possible combinations in terms of the relationship between the productive elements and the aspects of place and time.

In every design of work you are making assumptions about the relationship between the elements of productivity and the choices of place and time. You can hear these assumptions when the leadership team at Goldman Sachs say they want everyone working in the office, or the senior team at CPP Investments say that people can work anywhere for three months a year. The Goldman Sachs team are putting co-located place (the office) at the centre of their design, whilst the team at CPP Investments are thinking about the impact of distributed place (away from the office) and asynchronous time (disconnected from others).

What combination of time and place best supports each of the elements of productivity for your company? This is a question I have been directing my research towards for some years and in Figure 8,

	Energy	Focus	Coordination	Cooperation
Co-located (Office)	●	●	●	●
PLACE				
Distributed (Home)	●	●	●	●
Synchronous	●	●	●	●
TIME				
Asynchronous	●	●	●	●

Figure 7. Framework: The potential choice and impact of place/time and productivity.

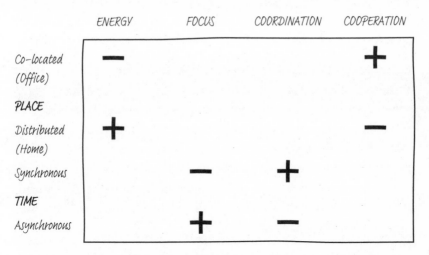

Figure 8. Framework: The impact of place and time on productivity.

I illustrate my view of this. Note that in the figure the impact can have both upsides (+) and downsides (–). This is important because it gives a sense of the trade-offs that have to be made.

Imagining the impact of place on energy and cooperation

UPSIDES

The choice of place (co-located or distributed) essentially impacts the energy and cooperation elements of productivity. Working in a *distributed* way, for example from home, boosts energy because you are able to pull back commuting time and assign it instead to physical energy-boosting activities such as sports and recreation, and emotional energy-boosting activities such as spending time with family and friends. Working in a *co-located* place, such as the office, boosts cooperation through the impact of face-to-face encounters and the possibility of serendipity as people bump into each other. This is driven by the network ties, and especially the distribution of weak ties we looked at in the network framework (Figure 4).

DOWNSIDES

Yet there are downsides that mirror these upsides. Working from home can shrink your social networks and the lack of face-to-face encounters with your colleagues can together reduce your cooperative productivity. Working from the office can deplete energy in part through the energy-sapping experiences of commuting, which can add two or three hours to the day and mean getting up early in the morning and arriving home exhausted late at night. And sitting at an office desk for hours at a time and eating junk-food lunches can reduce your health and vitality.

Imagining the impact of time *on focus and coordination*

UPSIDES

When your working time is *synchronized* (for example, everyone is working nine to five) then you have the chance to be connected to your colleagues and this boosts the productive element of coordination because of the natural synchronization of time between workers. For example, if you are all synchronized then without prior planning you can simply assume that everyone on your team can speak together at a certain time either virtually or face to face. This synchronization of time makes the coordination of tasks a great deal easier. When you work in an *asynchronized* way – and disconnected from others – then the impact is on potentially boosting the productive element of focus if you have created blocks of time in which you can really concentrate on the task at hand.

DOWNSIDES

But again there are downsides that mirror the upsides. When you are synchronizing your time with others then in a sense you are 'always on' and connected to others. That depletes your focus as it's likely you will be frequently interrupted. And when time is asynchronous and you are disconnected from others then your ability to coordinate can suffer because there is limited time, or even no time, when you and your colleagues can naturally, without prior agreement, work in tandem.

So, in redesigning work your aim is to maximize the upsides, minimize the downsides and manage the trade-offs. You can do this by imagining the office as a place of cooperation, the home as a source of energy, asynchronous time as a period of focus and synchronous, connected time as the basis of coordination.

Action #5
Reimagine place and time

- Take another look at the job families and the sources of productivity from Action #1 (page 26) and consider for each of these sources of productivity the likely configuration of place and time that will best support and boost productivity.
- The results of Action #3, 'understand what people want' (page 50), will help you to consider whether there are groups for whom this configuration might be suboptimal.
- It's important to weigh the trade-offs that these configurations are likely to create . . .
- . . . and to identify the prime time/place configuration and consider how best to optimize and how others are approaching this.

Reimagine place: The office as a space of cooperation

Since the Industrial Revolution, offices – those places of collective endeavour – have embodied the way we work. As you reimagine work there may be employees for whom being in an office would really boost cooperation. How might you do that? During the pandemic there was both demonization of the office – a terrible place we did not want to visit – but also glorification – a wonderful place where all sorts of encounters that created innovation took place. Of course, the reality was somewhere between the two as a short history of the office shows.

A short history of the office

My guess is that if you have ever worked in an office you have vivid memories of the first time you stepped inside one. I encountered mine in 1980 when, as a newly qualified psychology postgrad, I joined British Airways as a selection methods officer, or SMO. My boss, the SSMO (I will leave you to figure out that title) and his boss both had walled offices with views, whilst I inhabited a small room bathed in fluorescent light. In the 1980s BA, like most other large corporations, was a very hierarchical workplace, reflected in the numerous levels of job titles and the arrangements of the office. I was out and into a consultancy practice by 1985, with my own office and a view. Around me in the office the density had increased and the size of the cubicles shrunk.

Over the next couple of decades the design of offices became more open, with the aim of encouraging collaboration and teamwork. I can still remember my shock in 2004 when visiting John Browne, then the CEO of BP in the company's central London HQ. At the time, I was writing a case about the 'peer assist' organizational process at the firm and had come to BP to interview him.[1] I was directed to the top floor of the office block and told, 'The CEO will be sitting in the middle of the floor.' And indeed he was. In an open-plan office filled with desks, John Browne's was located in the centre – though I do recall he'd surrounded himself with a forest of potted greenery and a small army of pre-Columbian statues. He might have been in an open-plan office but, like many people, he valued his privacy.

On many office floors, particularly those inhabited by know-ledge workers, the open-plan office was replacing the cubicle. In fact, designers tell me that from around 1995 the height of cubicle walls dropped from sixty-five inches, to forty-eight, then thirty-six, finally disappearing altogether to be replaced by contiguous desks. This push in part reflected organizational skills and structures – knowledge workers were more important and cross-disciplinary teams more prevalent. Indeed, if you'd wandered into one of the tech-company offices you might find, as the designer Verda Alex-ander described to business media magazine *Fast Company* in 1991, 'skateboard ramps with DJ turntables, lots of game rooms with pool and ping-pong tables; we did music rooms and cafeterias with sophisticated barista bars and beer taps'.[2]

Open-plan offices were in vogue, and as offices opened up so the amount of space allocated to an employee shrank. In 2010 the average US employee had 200 square feet; by 2017 it had shrunk to 130 square feet. Understandably, those of us in open offices compensated for this erosion of personal space by building sound barriers with headphones. In a 2019 study, Harvard Business School's Ethan Bernstein and Humanyze President Ben Waber used smartphones and sensors to track face-to-face and digital interaction. They studied two Fortune 500 companies both before and after they moved from cubicles to open office. As they reported, 'We found that face-to-face interactions dropped by roughly 70 per cent after the firms transitioned to open office, while electronic interactions increased to compensate.' The virtual workplace, instead of complementing the physical one, had become a refuge from it.[3] It is important to remember that, even before the pan-demic, digital collaborative tools had already enabled workers to come into the office and spend all day online rarely talking to each other face to face.

So, as you go about reimagining what an office could be, you have a chance to really dial up the capacity of the office as a place of cooperation. How will you do this?

Be aware of the deep ambivalence to the office

The pandemic revealed a simple truth – we are deeply ambivalent about offices and being in them. We love spending less time in the office, but we fret about what this will mean for our future. This ambivalence was apparent even at the early stages of the pandemic. On 15 March 2020 I asked the 3,000 participants of a London Business School webinar I was conducting how they were feeling. To get sense of this I gave a selection of descriptions – one of which was 'OK, but I am missing my colleagues'. About 33 per cent of the webinar participants chose this response. This was only two weeks into lockdown and already people could feel the social connectivity with others beginning to fray.

There was much talk in those early stages of the pandemic of Stanford professor Nicholas Bloom's experiment in 2010–11 with call-centre workers in the Chinese travel company Ctrip (now Trip.com). At the time, his was one of the few experimental procedures that had empirically examined relative productivity in home and office work. In the experiment, half the call-centre workers remained in the office whilst the others worked at home for four days a week.[4] Bloom found a productivity uplift for those working from home, in part (as we discovered during the pandemic) because homeworkers tended to work longer hours. Interestingly, however, when, after nine months of being at home, these workers had the chance to come back to the office, around half of them chose to do so, even though many had daily commutes of over eighty minutes.

Also interesting is the earlier experience of IBM and Yahoo. By 2009 around 40 per cent of IBM's workforce were working remotely. In 2017, with profits falling, the company delivered an ultimatum: everyone must return to the office or leave the company. At Yahoo, Marissa Mayer, shortly after becoming CEO in 2012, had told all its 12,000 employees they could no longer work from home because innovation and collaboration were suffering. Not everyone was happy to comply, and by 2016 about a third of those affected had left the company.

Listen to people's dream of the perfect office

It's worth asking people in the company to describe their perfect office. The word 'office' is associated with a physical place – desks and computers, task lights, water coolers, coffee machines, cubicles, noise-cancelling partitions. But for all of us it's a lot more than a physical space. This was clear when I asked people on 15 March 2020 how they felt – it was not the office itself that they missed, it was the people. And in a sense, when we think about how work is designed, we've often conflated place (the office) and people (our colleagues, teams and customers). The office is essentially a co-located space.

So, the question you are faced with as you grapple with redesigning work is: What is an office for, and what is the perfect office? This was a question I put to members of my Future of Work Consortium. A selection of comments from the word cloud are shown on the following page.

What will it take to create this perfect office? Here are two suggestions: broaden your idea to reimagine the office as shared offices, satellites and hubs, and maximize the cooperative opportunities.

Insight: How Fujitsu reimagined the office

The question of office design was very much on the minds of the executive team at Fujitsu as they moved the majority of their workers in Japan from the office to the home during the pandemic. They realized they had a once in a lifetime chance to reimagine the spaces that some employees would return to. As they imagined what this could be, one thing was clear. A single type of office would no longer be appropriate, they needed to think beyond the one-size-fits-all model. Some of the design team had been members of my Future of Work Consortium for many years, and it was the model of networks and knowledge flows shown in Figure 4 that was one

Depicts the culture.

Precious time for collaboration and creation.

Breakout spaces with good acoustics.

Social meetings.

Not open plan.

Lots of space for collaboration.

Calm bright space.

Full of people.

Dog friendly.

Close to my home.

Bright, colourful and a space to chat and relax.

Lots of workshop/collaboration space.

Homelike.

Coffee station in centre to draw people in.

Relaxed area with opportunity for private-area work.

Inspirational space to connect.

Light, outside space to walk and talk.

Set up to maximize number of happy collisions.

Minimal doors and obstacles to movement.

Beautiful and comfortable.

On top of a hill.

With a view.

Good coffee.

Bright, full of plants and colours.

With an integrated outdoor space.

Not noisy, natural oxygen.

People from different businesses working together.

Beautiful pictures on the walls.

of their inspirations to reimagining the place of work. They began to create an office typology shaped around people's specific tasks and the network flows of knowledge.

They figured that, whilst some people would be happy for focused tasks to take place at home, others would not. That is in part because apartments in Japan are often small, and those with children or older relatives around really struggled during lockdown to get work done. To understand this better, the leadership team embarked on the first step of the design process – 'Understand'. To do this they commissioned a series of employee surveys to understand more fully what people wanted. A pre-pandemic survey had shown that 74 per cent of employees considered the office to be the best place to work. In a follow-up survey in May 2020 only 15 per cent of Fujitsu employees considered the office the best place to work. Now 30 per cent preferred their home, whilst 55 per cent favoured a mix of home and office. It seemed that whilst many employees enjoyed working from home *some* of the time, few wanted to work from home *all* the time. But there was a real downside to going into a city-centre office with a two-hour commute. These were wasted hours and a real energy drain. And moreover, even if people did go into the office, as we know from earlier observations on open offices, they were often distracted by others around them.

So, as the Fujitsu design team moved into the 'Reimagine' stage they began to imagine what a perfect office could be. What they saw was there was not one perfect office, but three – each designed specifically around key productivity elements. I've shown this in Figure 9.

THE NEIGHBOURHOOD SHARED OFFICE

Whilst many Fujitsu employees appreciated no longer having to commute into a city-centre office, some found working from home distracting. Their perfect office would be a place that was quiet, equipped with a well-functioning internet connection and a printer – and, importantly, near their home. As the design team moved into the third stage of the design cycle, 'Model and Test',

	ENERGY	FOCUS	COORDINATION	COOPERATION
Neighbourhood, shared offices	No commute	Undisturbed		
Satellite offices	No commute		Face to face virtual	
Hub office			Face to face	Brainstorm

Figure 9. Framework: The elements of productivity and office types.

they began from spring 2020 to invest in spaces near the neighbourhood where their employees lived. These 'shared offices' were equipped with single-occupancy working cubicles, internet and printers. In order to maximize use, some of these shared spaces would be located in railway stations, which already had food halls and lounges. These could be used by any Fujitsu employee who lived locally. In the shared office people could work on tasks that required focus, use the connectivity and screens to set up asynchronous coordination meetings with others, or spend time on the Fujitsu virtual learning platform.

Such shared offices have the potential to build and reinforce stronger neighbourhood bonds. In the future, these hubs could grow so that suppliers and customers would also use them. Rather like a 'WeWork', but with more corporate opportunities for chance encounters with people in the same sector.

THE SATELLITE OFFICE

As the Fujitsu design team modelled the different types of office they realized that, whilst neighbourhood shared offices would cope with the issues of proximity to home, they could not be designed explicitly for knowledge to flow across and within teams. In fact, the model was that in these offices employees would work individually in cubicles uninterrupted by others.

So they began to model a second type of perfect office – this time built around the needs of people with a strong coordination element to their work. These would be built again near network nodes such as stations, but also within the suburbs of Tokyo and other large cities.

They would be for employees working in project teams, for example, who had to check in with their colleagues on a regular basis – perhaps once or twice a week. This is a place where project teams can book space and run their project meetings. Equipped with video conferencing and smart creative technologies and coffee stations, it's a place where people can go when they want to get together. These places would also be equipped for teams to meet virtually with access to Fujitsu's collaborative technology platforms for project check-up or document sign-offs.

THE HUB OFFICE

For significant, creative and innovate occasions Fujitsu's design team decided to create spaces that would be visually engaging and exciting. Places where colleagues and suppliers could meet, with brainstorm facilities, open space, access to fresh air. This was the hub office and it was designed to maximize cooperative opportunities.

Fujitsu – questions for reflection
Have you considered the location options that are most appropriate for the primary tasks in your key roles (energy, focus, coordination, cooperation)? Take a look at Figure 9 – the elements of productivity and office types. What types of office do you currently have? As you consider the redesign of work, which office type or types would be most appropriate?

Imagine the office as a place of cooperation

The office is many things – but fundamentally for most people it's a place of connections. A glance back to the networks diagram in Figure 4 (reproduced below) gives some of the clues as to the nature of those connections – a co-located space is a place of connectivity and a space that can support and encourage any, or all, of the network processes.

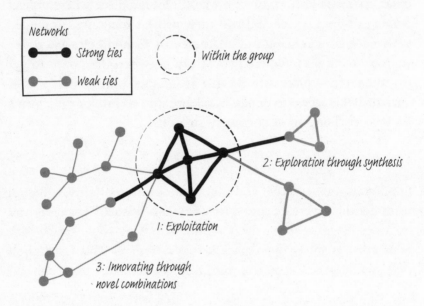

It can be a location where people who know each other well and are in the same group collectively *exploit* the tacit knowledge they possess as individuals. It's a space where people from more than one group who know each other well can deliberately meet in order to *explore through synthesis* what they know from their various experiences and perspectives.

And there is one other network that can be enormously important to a collective location – innovation through *novel combinations*, when people who do not know each other well, or perhaps not at all (the weak ties), randomly bump into each other. It's this syn-chronicity, these random 'water cooler' conversations, that can be the basis of something new and extraordinary.

Insight: How Arup uses the office to maximize cooperative opportunities

As with Fujitsu in Tokyo, the Arup design team for the com-pany's office in Melbourne had gone about purposefully designing places for cooperation. Jenni Emery, a senior executive, told me that she believed shared, communal spaces would always have a role:

> I do believe we will go back to physical offices eventually, but there
> needs to be a lot of thought about how those physical spaces will
> and should be used. They have been used really as a factory – a last
> vestige of the industrial revolution. We need to forget about that.
> They must be used to promote community, a place of collaboration.
> So, that is how we at Arup are working, thinking about networks
> and collaboration.

PLAYING WITH PROXIMITY

I also got a feel for this from Joe Correnza, who was part of the design team for Arup's iconic Melbourne HQ. Not surprisingly, as one of the leading design and architectural practices in the world, this is an office that gets as close to perfection as possible. Large sweeping views, broad staircases and wooden flooring combine to create a space that Correnza describes as 'a place for those ser-endipitous encounters – where designers mingle with architects and engineers'. He goes on to describe how they 'wanted to build collaborative spaces, reduce personal spaces and give back to collaboration – big tables, scribbling boards'. Large, airy spaces on the ground floor and open atriums encourage synergy. This diffu-sion of knowledge is about how teams work together. But it's also about proximity – who sits next to whom, the adjacencies between people. In order to make the most of these adjacent knowledge flows and diffusion, every four months the teams in the Melbourne office are physically moved to another part of the building with a view to creating new adjacencies. As Joe says, 'It was a great opportunity for people to hear and see others working – being proximate is a crucial driver to building relationships.'

BEING PART OF THE NEIGHBOURHOOD

What I found most compelling about the Arup office in Melbourne is the way it sits in its neighbourhood. In fact, that was one of the primary design briefs for it. As Joe explained, 'We wanted the space to be sufficiently transparent to break down the boundaries between "us" inside the office and "them" outside of the office.' And it's not just the space, but what happens within the space. The building is a magnet for activity, hosting a broad range of events that draw in the local community.

It has also become a catalyst for developing cooperative relationships with partners. As Joe told me:

> It's a space to welcome them. Our suppliers and partners can use this space, they can work here, use the café, sit in our space – we welcome the exchange. We also host industry events. In the first year, over 200 people a week came to visit the office with over 140 events. We want to be an open space – a node.

I asked Joe how a company without the mighty resources and design savvy of Arup could approach designing the office for cooperation. He had three ideas. First, aim to reduce the amount of personal space and be prepared to give this space back to become cooperative space. Next, encourage teams to meet as often as possible in the open space outside of meeting rooms, so that others can feel the buzz of the group. Finally, move groups of people every quarter to new seating so that they have the opportunity to meet new people.

A closing remark from Arup's Jenni Emery:

We believe we will still very much need workspaces in the future, as much as ever. We need them to have equality of space at work, to have those important encounters with each other, to exchange knowledge and learn. So much of learning comes from osmosis, by being alongside people. But, we need to be really intentional and considered about how we use offices in the future – and about how we use virtual space.

So, as you reimagine work one of the primary roles of the office will be as a place where new members of the business are socialized and learn about the place. As we will see, that is less about the actual space and more about the intentionality with which work is organized within it.

Arup – questions for reflection
Are there tasks as you think about the redesign of work that will require face-to-face cooperation? What are the spaces where this cooperation will take place? Is there anything that you can learn from Arup about how they maximize cooperation? On the question of proximity, is there more that you could do to maximize this valuable resource? Have you considered the role of the office in the community – is there more you could do to bring the 'outside in'?

Action #6
Reimagine the office as a place of cooperation

- First, imagine your office as a variety of spaces. Are there activities that require different spaces? Consider how Fujitsu developed shared offices, satellites and hubs.

- Next, in your office space, consider the flow of knowledge and information – is there a need for more open and circulation spaces?
- Then, imagine the groupings of people within the space – where teams sit, adjacencies and the possibility of moving people every four months.
- Finally, imagine the office space in its community and neighbourhood. Are there opportunities to bring the outside in and engage more closely with others?

Reimagine place: The home as a source of energy

We've had more than forty years' experience of technology-enabled homeworking. From the 1980s, fuelled by technological develop-ments, it was freelancers who became the era's social pioneers of virtual working. They used the early incarnations of personal computers to design products, build code, write and edit from their homes. They sold their services on an hourly or project basis to corporations without being a signed-up employee. Studies of freelancers tell us something about how this played out. From this group of early adopters we learnt that they loved the autonomy of managing their own time and the flexibility of where they worked.[5]

The pain and glory of homeworking

An experiment in 1992 by the executive team at the telecoms giant BT gave some early insights into the lessons of homeworking for their 'directory enquiries' call-centre workers. Half the teams were assigned to work from home and half from the office. In the spirit of experimentation, base-line data were collected from both groups: their engagement, performance and retention. Then, over a period of time, the performance of both the homeworking and the office-working groups was measured.

This turned out to be a very early lesson in experimental courage. Within weeks the performance of the homeworking group dipped. The internet connectivity let them down badly. They did not know how to coordinate with each other when they could no longer pop over to another cubicle to ask a question, and they felt disorientated and adrift. But in the spirit of determination and experimental protocol, the executive team gritted their teeth and resolved to see it through.

What they discovered was that over time the performance of the homeworkers increased. People began to learn how to make the technology work more to their advantage and created workarounds to the daily catch-ups in the office. And within a month it began to exceed that of the office-based workers. Those working from home felt more engaged because they valued the flexibility they now had. They spoke of being able to more easily look after their children or run errands. And, of course, those who no longer had a commute relished that extra time. Importantly, in an industry where retention is historically low, many more employees decided to stay in the job.

The experiment turned out to be a major turning point at BT, and by 2000 a significant portion of the workforce worked from home. More importantly, the knowledge and experience of these veteran homeworkers became crucial as the corporation swung more towards flexible working in jobs that were less routine than those early directory-enquiry assistants. As Dr Nicola Millard, the principal innovation partner at BT, told me – they learnt much from these veteran workers. In fact, in the early stages of the pandemic she created 'A practical guide to successful homeworking' – a document compiled from the many tips that veteran homeworkers had gleaned over the years: create a space that works for you; routine is everything; keep healthy and don't feel guilty for taking breaks; connect with colleagues through informal chats; make the experience less remote by using technologies effectively and many more.

Listen to people's ideas of their perfect homeworking space

It is worth stepping back for a moment to remind ourselves, and indeed to understand, what it is that people like when they are working from home. What is clear from data collected in many companies during the months of the pandemic was that the majority of people loved the chance to work from home and many want this option to be part of the redesign of work. They enjoyed the freedom and flexibility of homework and the chance to get to know their neighbours better. For many, pulling back from the daily commute had been a real eye opener. To understand this more deeply, in a webinar in mid 2021 I asked participants, 'How best could you energize working from home?' They let their imagination roam. The word cloud opposite shows some of their descriptions.

People described the chance to work from home as creating real opportunities to be energized: space to think; prepare healthy food; walk in the neighbourhood; see the family. As I talked to leaders, they too had experienced many of these same benefits – and from a corporate perspective they could see other advantages including reduced office costs, less physical and emotional wear and tear from long commutes and an opportunity to engage and retain staff.

Working from home can and will be a vital source of energy. But to do that, we need to learn from the past whilst also realizing that homeworking (which is essentially virtual work) has to have a whole host of intentional practices and processes in place to be truly successful.

Maintaining energy at home

In 1994 Cesare Marchetti, an Italian physicist, noted that, through history, humans have shown a willingness to spend roughly sixty minutes a day in transit. This explains why cities like Rome never exceeded about three miles in diameter. Steam trains, streetcars and cars expanded that distance – but transit times stayed the same. The

Light and space.

Regular breaks and walks.

Snacks.

Make my own lunches.

Dedicated
space
for me to work.

Quiet.

Break from
interruptions.

A space to think.

Peaceful and happy.

Able to squeeze in a workout.

Meditation.

Time to walk.

Views over a garden.

Comfortable
desk and
chair.

Healthy meals.

Access to outdoors.

Serendipity.

Nearby café
to walk to.

Structured day with transition periods.

Comfort and familiarity.

Music or silence.

Fresh air.

Regular and
deliberate
breaks.

My dog.

Healthy
food options.

Close to nature.

Flexibility.

Not worrying
about visibility.

Time to focus on personal things.

Control
over time.

Time to exercise.

Reliable
Wi-Fi.

Combine work with the family.

Natural behaviour.

Do what I like.

Door to close
to separate
personal and
work life.

Building a
neighbourhood
network.

Ask how the
family is.

Privacy.

Comfortable places to sit.

Be home
on time.

Being able to keep on top of my caring responsibilities.

one-way average for an American commute stands at about twenty-seven minutes.[6]

When we commute we are in a sense using that time to cross from one identity to another. This crossing from one identity to another is what psychologists call 'boundary work'.[7] When we leave home for work we initiate a sequence where we are in a sense deactivating our feelings about home and replacing them with feelings about work. When this 'boundary work' does not happen, we experience 'role spillover', and this makes it more difficult to concentrate and creates more stress at home and in work.

This role spillover was compounded for many homeworkers with the distractions they experienced at home. The veteran homeworkers at BT had already described that one of the downsides of working from home was being distracted – by children, flatmates, elderly parents. For homeworkers with young children at home during the pandemic, this had been particularly tough. In a webinar I ran on 14 March 2020 over 10 per cent of the nearly 3,000 people polled said their most significant experience of homeworking was being distracted. Of course, this was a time when children were at home rather than at school, but even as we returned to more normal family lives we still had caring responsibilities – children on holiday, looking after older relatives or people with disabilities. That's why it's so important that, as we redesign work, we learn from these experiences and put these new learnings into practice in the years to come.

What many newly homebound workers had begun to realize is something psychologists had studied for decades, which is that when it comes to distractions, boundaries really matter.[8] What these intensive home-based ways of working revealed with absolute clarity was just how important boundary management can be. Imagine for a moment a day in the life of Riley, a sales manager in a medium-sized consulting firm. Here is a typical (pre-pandemic) working day: she leaves her family and home in the morning to commute for ninety minutes into the office. In both her home and her work domain she has a separate identity. When she is in the home domain she is the caring mother. When she is in the work domain she's a hard-hitting sales person. These two identities are distinct from each other. When she's a sales executive this is in a sense an inflexible, impermeable role that requires her full attention and concentration. When being a mother she is caring, patient, empathic. So as she moves from one role identity to the other she is making a significant and potentially tense transition.

One of the ways Riley (and most other executives in these types of role) manage the potentially significant tension between these two domains is to create boundaries. These are often symbolic activities that create a *rite of passage* between the two identities and include props such as putting on her business suit, or activities like boarding the commuter train, having a pre-meeting coffee or catching up with the news. These cue her new identity, signal the role shift and ensure fewer cross-role interruptions. When she assumes her sales role she no longer thinks about being a mum because she's psychologically compartmentalized these roles, and when she assumes her mum role she no longer (theoretically) thinks about being a sales executive. Of course, in principle the devices she carries with her from the managerial to the mum role bring the work right into the home – particularly if she struggles with being 'always on' and connected.

In theory, the boundary transitions we make from one identity to another serve to enhance our performance in each role and help preserve our distinct selves. I've shown how this occurs in Figure 10. Some transitions are *physical*, such as the shift from being at home and working in the office. Some are *cognitive* shifts, for example separating worrying about whether a child's lunch box has been packed with healthy food from calculating the monthly sales figures. Other shifts are *relational*, for example separating talking to a child about being bullied at school from mentoring a young member of the work team. Some are *temporal* shifts, time when one activity (e.g. looking after the children) is regulated and bounded from another activity (e.g. working on a project).

When these boundaries are maintained, they significantly reduce

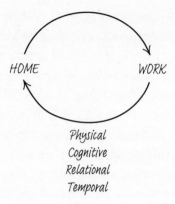

Figure 10. Framework: Boundary management.

the potential blurring between being 'on' for one role and 'off' for the other. And as a result, people are less distracted. Yet these boundaries come at a cost. It can be tough if there is a significant transition between two segmenting roles, for example being assertive at work and caring at home.

To understand this, take Cameron, a father who for some years has tutored dyslexic children, both online occasionally from his home office and sometimes face to face at a local healthcare centre.

It is worth noting that, whilst Riley's two identities (sales executive and mother) are highly segmented in the sense they require some very different attributes, Cameron's two identities are much more integrated. For both roles he performs (counsellor and father) overlapping attributes of caring and empathy are salient. As a consequence, he is not making the sort of psychological shift that Riley is.

However, that does not make it any easier for Cameron. As a parent, often working from home, there are interruptions and these are frequently unpredictable: he is counselling in his home office when one of the children comes in and asks what's for lunch; as he is talking with a patient he is wondering whether his child is completing their homework. The benefit for Cameron is that, because the boundaries he is crossing are to a similar role, there is not the transitional energy drain that Riley has to endure. But the downside is that, without this clear psychological and cognitive boundary, he is interrupted very often and each time he is interrupted it takes time for his mind to reconnect with the work he was engaged in.

Now imagine that in the redesign of work Riley is working from her home two days a week whilst Cameron continues to move between home, office and health centre. What should Riley and Cameron do?

The veterans from the early homeworking experiments at BT had good advice – routine is everything; keep healthy and don't feel guilty for taking breaks; connect with colleagues through informal chats; make the experience less remote by using technologies effectively. And what psychologists who study transitions and homeworking also emphasize is 'establish and control your boundaries'.

How might you, in the redesign of work, support homeworkers to establish and maintain their boundaries?

REPLICATE TRANSITIONS

For a start, those working from home looking to reduce distractions and establish boundaries would be wise to replicate the transitions and boundaries they've probably established when they went from home to work. That means maintaining physical boundaries by moving to a new room when they are working and erecting what researchers have called 'default idiosyncratic boundaries'. Riley already had these at her work office – actively creating her own space, with her own stuff that shows who she is.

Studies of people's homeworking spaces show how idiosyncratic they are. Just glancing at my own home office, I see that it is piled with books, with a desk and a makeshift table that we often used for children's parties along one wall – again piled with books. There are family photographs lying around the place, a green screen dominates one wall, and I can see an array of shoes scattered around – just out of camera view. Yet when I walk into this small room and close the door I step into a new identity with new cues. Both you and your employees will have to create their own idiosyncratic space.

And then it would be wise to consider replicating the behaviour cues that helped Riley make the transition from home to office. To understand this, think about how you make the transition yourself – putting on business attire, perhaps taking a train, almost certainly drinking coffee. When you are working from home you are spared this lengthy transition. But in its place, it is important to create similar if less elaborate rituals that will stimulate the identity switch. For me, it's going downstairs to the kitchen to make a cup of coffee that I bring up to my study. Often I take a few gulps of fresh air in the garden and check whether anything needs watering. Then it's down to work.

REGULATE SPACE AND TIME

Crucially, homeworkers have to learn to regulate access to their space and their time. They need to engage in what researchers have called 'boundary work'.[9] And if we are to be productive in our new working lives, then this will be a core competency for all of us. It turns out that the more blurred the lines between our identities, and the more we are juggling activities, then the greater the negative impact such strains place on job satisfaction and engagement. Solving this means regulating access to place and time – both the physical workspace in terms of restricting access to others and, with regard to time, rescheduling domestic tasks and setting specific periods when others can connect.

MAKE TEAM AGREEMENTS

Creating temporal boundaries is crucial. Homeworkers have, as much as possible, to reduce the random nature of interruptions. That's because it is randomness that has the biggest negative impact on focus, concentration and performance. That means negotiating with family members when they are 'available'. And, more importantly, regulating access to time by the company and colleagues. Teams have set about this in a number of ways. One is team agreements, where members agree in advance when they are available for team catch-ups and team meetings, and when they need focused time to concentrate, for example on writing a client report or preparing sales figures.

HOW YOUR COMPANY CAN ENCOURAGE BOUNDARIES

There is also much that your business can do to support employees to manage their boundaries. To learn more about this, in April 2020 my advisory group HSM Advisory held a seven-day open platform 'hackathon' where executives could talk to each other about their experiences and brainstorm solutions. People joined from more than thirty companies in Europe, the US, Japan, Australia and New Zealand. At that time more than 60 per cent were working from home with family responsibilities (that percentage was about the norm for many countries). They described three ways of thinking about this: understand the employee's specific circumstances, empathize with their reality and ramp up technology.

Many felt that in order to support homeworkers, executives needed to start by understanding their employee's often idiosyncratic situation. As one executive commented, 'Do you really know who your people are? We realized that our stereotypical family was way off the mark – there are many varieties of families; it's wrong to generalize.' This understanding makes it easier to empathize with the reality of people working from home with caring responsibility. I heard how in one company this meant encouraging leaders to tell their own stories about working from home and sharing the distractions that they experienced. They wanted people to be open about the tensions and challenges they faced – however senior their roles. Others talked about the importance of focusing on 'moments that matter', times when getting the right type of support made a disproportionate impact. Take, for example, a moment that matters when a child becomes sick. How the team and manager either offer support or fail to empathize has a lasting impact on how the working parent feels about the company. As one manager commented, 'If you can get this right, there are real benefits for engagement and loyalty.'

And, as BT's veterans showed, there are real gains by using technology to ensure boundaries are established between 'on' time, when they were available to respond and collaborate with others, and 'off' time, when they could engage in energy-boosting activities. That meant, for example, taking proper lunch breaks and making sure they symbolically 'left their workplace' at the end of the day. They also negotiated boundaries with family and colleagues so these boundaries would hold up.

But beyond all of these ways of supporting homeworkers was the overriding view that it was crucial to focus performance management on outcomes, not presenteeism.

Insight: How BT and TCS focus on outcomes not 'presenteeism'

If home is going to be an energizing place then you have to confront one significant source of anxiety – that if people choose to work from home they are less likely to be promoted.

It is easy to underestimate the significant role that proximity plays in keeping people top of mind. At home you can feel that you are out of sight. Indeed, one of the main drivers of being 'always on' is captured in the letters FOMO (fear of missing out), and what people are most fearful of missing out on is promotion and a pay rise.

It does not have to be like this, and there is much we can learn from companies that historically have a large distributed workforce. They describe three important lessons: focusing intentionally on outcomes, agreeing performance outcomes in the teams and trusting people.

Interestingly, when I quizzed BT's Nicola Millard about this, she told me that there was no difference between promotion rates in BT for homeworkers vs office workers.

What is clear is that, left unresolved, out of sight can be out of mind. Overcoming this anxiety will require you to engage in some intentional work design. Often the sticking point is how to support and measure performance.

FOCUS INTENTIONALLY ON OUTCOMES

I was intrigued by how BT had ensured there were no differences in the promotion rates of home and office workers. Nicola Millard explained: 'Promotion has not been a problem. We don't have a culture around presenteeism. Many people are not co-located with their manager, often they don't meet. We are quite a remote organization with a distributed workforce, so being seen in an office and face to face regularly is rare.' I asked her how, with this distributed workforce, performance was managed. She described BT's intentional design of work: 'There are regular team meetings, check-ins and one-to-ones. Importantly, every month everyone writes a report to their manager. It's a brief about what they have done that month.' I was interested in how, under these conditions, executives are able to get a sense of comparative performance, let's say between three managers. As Nicola told me, 'We've really learnt that focusing on outcomes rather than being present in the office is crucial.'

At Tata Consultancy Services, working virtually has been part of the company culture and practices from the very beginning. With around 500,000 employees across forty-six countries and 154 nationalities, the focus has always been on how to work across the world whilst delivering customer satisfaction and business performance.

The TCS executive team are among the founding partners of my Future of Work Consortium, joining in 2009 and partnering on a series of research initiatives. Like BT, they have a history of distributed working. I asked them how they thought about managing performance under these conditions. They have taken the approach of emphasizing outcomes rather than being present. As Ramkumar Chandrasekaran, who heads the consultancy's HR function in the UK, told me, 'Our enterprise-wide platforms help us to build strong collaboration practices. These include deciding upfront on goals and key roles; clearly defining boundaries and spans of control; clarifying tasks and processes; and measuring roles and commitments.'

TRUST PEOPLE

Designing work that can be done virtually comes down to practices and processes. Importantly, it is also about values. In my conversation with the TCS executives they emphasized the importance of focusing on values. For them, trust is key. They have to trust that people working from home are engaged and productive. As they eloquently put it, 'Trust someone until they have been proven untrustworthy.'

BT and TCS – questions for reflection
Considering the way these two companies went about this aspect of redesigning work, do you have data that suggest people who are working from home are concerned that they will not be promoted as fast as those working from the office? Have you found any evidence of this? As you consider this issue take a closer look at how performance is measured and assessed. Is there more you can do to ensure that you are measuring outcomes?

BE AWARE OF THE DEEP GENDER DYNAMICS OF HOMEWORKING

Our experiences during the pandemic opened a window on the home. For some this was a warning sign about what the impact of long-term homeworking could be. Anne Boden, who is the CEO and founder of Starling Bank, has said, 'I think we've gone through this great realization that many people are far more effective working from home.' However, she warns that women could be penalized if firms fail to strike the right balance between working in the office and from home, saying, 'We could end up in a situation where some people work in an office and get great opportunities, while others in the regions, older people, women with caring responsibilities, shoulder a lot of the workload but get none of the glory.'

Let's take a look at this with the experiences of two parents as they negotiated working from home rather than working in the office.

First, years of research data show that the probability in a male/female partnership is that the woman will do more domestic labour (cleaning the clothes, shopping and cooking, childcare and so on) than the man.[10] And even if the woman earns more than her partner, it's probable that she still does more work than him in the home. Earlier we looked at how being distracted can break concentration – and because women typically perform more domestic labour, they are more likely to be distracted. And that's compounded because, whilst men tend to do the predictable, routine tasks (such as every week taking out the rubbish or washing the car), women do many of the less routine, unpredictable tasks (such as taking a child to the doctor, or shopping for new shoes). There is more: whilst women are more likely to be interrupted and disturbed, they are also likely to do more of the cognitive, behind-the-scenes tasks that require a daily mental 'checklist'. Ensuring, for example, that the kids are having a healthy diet, planning the week's shopping to ensure it is balanced, checking in that the children are getting on with their friends.

So as homeworking becomes more prevalent, how can we ensure that it's a source of energy for women as well as for men?

It turns out the answer to this is not straightforward. As one executive remarked to me, there are real challenges in homeworking: 'This simply bakes in the gender inequality we have already been experiencing.' As they went on to describe, 'The challenge is that, faced with a choice of working from home or working in the office, it is mothers of small children who will overwhelmingly make this choice. And by doing so bake in the feminization of homeworking. And the upshot is that they will be less likely to be promoted.'

An executive shared with me another aspect of this dilemma:

People are moving towards their own idiosyncratic working solutions. As a company, our view has been that we ask people to perform a task and outside of that give them freedom. It is up to them to reassign their time between home and work. But what is happening is that women are spending many more (unpaid) hours working in the home, so when decisions are taken around who earns the most, their career needs can be discounted. We want to create equity between people who have kids and those who do not. But we acknowledge that there is no way that this equity is naturally created when people make different life choices. That is where the broader diversity and inclusion policies step in – we want to be open and fair. And if you as an executive team have not worked on these issues – now is the moment to get a lot of things right.

What would it take to redesign work to get a lot of things right? Professor Aneeta Rattan, a colleague of mine at London Business School and a prominent scholar in diversity and gender studies,[11] told me what she thought the priorities for the redesign of work should be so that gender differences aren't compounded:

The major intervention a company can do now is to acknowledge the reality of the situation and that it requires concessions on the part of both men and women in terms of household tasks and responsibility. They need to implement procedures that allow them to do their jobs. It's about giving time to people. It is for the collective good.

She added:

Couples need to reconceptualize what a work day looks like and recreate a set of norms that communicate a more equal assumption of household work. For example, we know you cannot work an eight-hour day in a dual-working couple – neither of you can do this. So develop time frameworks to help you do this. For example, together you work an eight-hour day, but each of you works for four hours and does four hours' childcare. So select the weekly block of four hours and work with your team to schedule these hours.

That means working flexibly. So whilst the household does the same amount of working hours, it is split between both partners. When I spoke to executives about how they could make this work they talked about the crucial importance of signalling the 'new norms'. For example, it's fine if you are on a call and the kids come into the room. Aneeta is clear that corporations can play a key role by providing guidelines, frameworks and tools for parents and carers to understand and work around their situation.

Another alternative is splitting the time, not with someone in your household, but with another person. That's the basic principle of role-sharing – where two people perform one job with well-developed coordinating mechanisms in place to enable both to perform. As we will explore later, a range of platforms have been developed to match job-shares with each other, and then to the job.

IMAGINE HOMEWORKING AS AN OPPORTUNITY TO EXPLORE REAL-WORLD NEIGHBOURHOODS

Redesigning work around the home creates exciting opportunities to reinvigorate neighbourhoods. During the pandemic many of us discovered our networks pivoted from work colleagues to neighbourhood friendships. With more time at home we were able to explore our neighbourhood. We might not be bumping into work colleagues in the office, but we are bumping into neighbours in our community. And who is to know whether the serendipity created by these chance encounters might be just as valuable as office meetings?

That renewed focus on neighbourhood communities has been the experience of Christy Johnson and her team at Artemis

Connection. She discovered that, with more time spent working from home, Artemis employees volunteered more in their community and became more involved with their neighbours.

So, as we redesign work and engage the home more in the domain of work, there is a chance not only to reduce commuting time but also to potentially create benefits to communities. This could be crucial to combating the isolation that sociologist Robert Putnam described in his book *Bowling Alone*.[12] He studied the history of bowling clubs from the 1950s and described how at that time in many suburban American towns, ten-pin bowling was a pivotal community activity as teams of people came together for friendly matches with other teams. And inevitably, because these teams represented many strata of society – from tradesmen to professionals like lawyers and doctors – these clubs also brought people together, creating along the way empathy and understanding for others. They built, in other words, what was called 'social capital' – the networks of friendships and reciprocity that connected people in neighbourhoods together. But from the 1950s onwards these bowling teams began to disband. Their members now commuted into the nearby cities, worked longer hours and had less free time at home – they simply did not have the flexibility to bowl at specific times in their neighbourhood teams. And with the demise of community activities like bowling clubs came the winding down of social capital and the increase of isolation.

The redesign of work has the potential to reverse this trend and build stronger neighbourhood social capital. It can do this by creating greater flexibility and more leisure time as people working from home can seize back their commuting hours. Christy Johnson has found that, as her colleagues work from home, so they often use that extra time and flexibility to build stronger bonds with their community.

She gave me examples of what people do: serving on the city council, being a governing board member on a citizens' climate-change council, teaching at university, doing non-profit board work, volunteering in their child's school, joining Tech Coast Angels, being entrepreneur in residence at a volunteering neighbourhood association, joining Women in Music.

These are just some of the ways that people can spend more time in their communities when they have time and flexibility.

The complex topic of homeworking and sustainability

As we go about redesigning work, one of the questions we will be asking is whether these new ways of working will positively impact on the drive for sustainability. Will they lead to a reduction of an individual's and a business's carbon footprint?

On the face of it there is much to celebrate about the redesign of work – less commuting and reduced business travel both have the potential to reduce the carbon footprint. But as I learnt from Alexandru Dinca, who is Unilever's Employee Experience global sustainability lead, whilst there is much to celebrate, the realities are more complex. Unilever is a global manufacturer of foods and personal care products and Alex is a member of a cross-functional Employee Experience team that focuses on designing and providing solutions for the company's 149,000 employees and aims to make their work experience simpler and better. The team includes members with roles touching on business travel and fleet, workplace design and safety, facilities, HR services, recruitment, IT platforms and technologies and global mobility, among others. Alex's role in the team is to ensure that, as far as possible, the 'employee experience' is sustainable. With regard to redesigning work, he found there are a number of factors that have to be taken into consideration in the redesign if reducing the carbon footprint is a priority.

COMMUTING – IT DEPENDS ON THE MODE OF TRANSPORT

As Alex remarked:

When people started to work from home it was everyone's first thought that with no commuting, the carbon footprint would drop. But in reality, on an average within a global company 80 per cent of office-based employees work within ten to twenty kilometres of their home and in developed countries most use public transport. Those in developing countries – particularly when they are in cities with poor public transport – tend to use their own cars . . . So [their carbon footprint] depends on how people commute. It's zero if they are walking, biking, using electric transport like the Tube/BEVs [battery-powered electric vehicles]; it is low/medium if they are taking a bus, car sharing, or using a hybrid car; and it's medium/high if they are solo driving in oil-fuelled cars.

So, what is important to consider is that when people are commuting into the office, you encourage them as much as possible to use low-energy travel solutions.

WORKING FROM HOME – IT DEPENDS WHETHER THE HOME IS ENERGY EFFICIENT

Again, the carbon footprint from homeworking is not straightforward – the difference between the office and the home depends on the energy efficiency levels of the home and of the office. In many developed countries such as the US or Japan, home-workers on average occupy homes that are 20 per cent *more* carbon intensive than the office. That's because in these countries there has been much focus on reducing the energy consumption of offices, factories and depots. However, there are some regions – such as the Scandinavian countries – where governments significantly subsidize homeowners to reduce the carbon footprint of their home (e.g. by supporting solar panels), whilst in many developing countries (Nigeria being one example) homes are highly energy inefficient and can use between 80 and 100 per cent more carbon than offices. So, as you consider your company's carbon footprint you will need to assess the footprint of those homes used for working as well as offices and factories.

THE BIG IMPACT – BUSINESS AIR TRAVEL

Face-to-face meetings will always have an important role, but as Alex told me, 'Reducing air travel is the biggest opportunity for decreasing the carbon footprint as you redesign work. Currently in most aircraft, the carbon cost per passenger flight (with a four-hour average flight time) is one ton of CO_2. Compare that with rail travel – which if the rail system is electrified and running on renewable energy is zero cost.' So, as you go about redesigning work, factor in the impact of air travel – make sure that every business trip is really crucial – and where possible, encourage train rather than air travel.

YOUNG PEOPLE ARE LEADING THE WAY

One fascinating point Alex made was that workers who are under the age of thirty use in general 25 per cent less energy. Why might this be? Alex points to three main factors:

> First, they tend to live alone or only with a partner – they have not yet had children. Next, they tend to be more technology driven and, in their choices, buy goods that are more energy efficient and intelligent – for example, an air conditioner that uses less energy by blowing air only where / when it is needed. And finally, young people often prefer to work from home and in choosing where to live, want to rent or buy homes that are less utility intensive, better insulated and have better access to renewable energy.

So as you go about factoring in the impact of your model for work on the carbon footprint be sure to encourage the voices of younger employees to be heard. Ultimately, Alex underlines the power of crowdsourcing of ideas to better understand the big challenges and opportunities that we are faced with to assess and tackle the CO_2 impact of working from home.

> *Reducing your carbon footprint – questions for reflection*
> Do you have any data about the carbon footprint of running your business offices? How does it compare with home-working? What impact will the redesign of work have on commuting, working from home, business air travel? And as you think about how to gain real momentum, is there more you can do to enable young people to be champions of sustainability in your business?

Action #7
Reimagine the home as a source of energy

- Take a closer look at your current homeworking veterans. What have you learnt from them? And, take a look also at the experience of homeworking during the pandemic. What did people like and what did they see as the trade-offs? Are there ways of mitigating these trade-offs?
- As you focus on the practices and processes that help homeworkers to establish and maintain boundaries, is there more you can do to send out a stronger message about expectations and try to shift the norms? Consider in particular physical, cognitive, relational and temporal boundaries.
- For homeworkers, examine how performance is managed. Is there sufficient focus on outcomes to enable homeworkers to avoid the negative aspects of 'presenteeism'?
- Consider the experiences of men and women working from home. Are you inadvertently reinforcing the gender dynamics that require women to shoulder more of the burden of domestic tasks? Should you have a more open

conversation about this and reconsider the policies around flexible working times?

- What are the steps you can take to ensure that homeworking does not inadvertently increase the carbon footprint of your firm?

Reimagine time: Creating focus with asynchronous time

Place is usually considered to be the primary aspect in redesigning work. That was particularly evident during the pandemic when hundreds of newspaper column inches were devoted to the home/office debate. But if you concentrate solely on place, you are overlooking a second, very important aspect – time. In the everyday experience of work it is often the distribution and design of time that creates the rhythm and cadence of the working day, week and month.

Let's take a look first at asynchronous time, periods when we are disconnected and therefore have the possibility of being productive by focusing on the task in hand.

Being focused is especially crucial for knowledge workers – think back to the investment analysts at CPP Investments, poring over company data and research reports and then synthesizing and preparing a cogent report. This focused time provides opportunities for them to recommend investment decisions that could be significant to the performance of the company.

What is it that we are doing when we engage in focused work? If you are to redesign work to enhance focus, then it makes sense to learn a little more about the nature of how and when humans focus.

Machines and humans focus differently

We can see this by contrasting human focus with that of machines. That's an important comparison, because over time machine performance will substitute for more focused human work. Yet despite this, the human capacity to focus will actually become more rather than less important, and understanding that can give us some clues about how to design work for focus. To explain this apparent contradiction we need to zoom out to consider the universal trends in machines and automation and how these are likely to develop over the coming years.

Right now what cognitive machines – those using artificial intelligence (AI) or machine learning – are adept at is scanning and analysing vast amounts of data. They achieve this at a scale and speed that the human brain cannot compete with. Through this process of scanning, machines are able to perform multiple correlations on vast data sets to reveal the underlying relationships within the data. The world first became aware of this in 1989, when the IBM machine named *Deep Blue* beat the reigning world chess champion Garry Kasparov. The machine did this by permutating the consequences of all possible moves at any point, and then comparing these possible moves with a data set created from past games. Kasparov was performing the same mental mapping: he too was imagining the next set of moves against his own knowledge of past games gained from watching others and reading chess manuals describing the winning moves of former chess masters. The success of *Deep Blue* resulted from the machine's ability to perform these computational tasks faster than its human opponent, and to have 'memorized' more past moves. And since the 1990s, in games such as chess, machines invariably beat humans.

That's even true of the game Go – considered one of the most complex board games. With 180 blue and 180 white stones arrayed across a 19×19 board, there are millions of possible configurations. In 2016 a machine using a program built by DeepMind, *AlphaGo*, played the South Korean world champion Lee Sedol in a series of five games in Seoul. It won four out of the five games. Subsequently, Lee helped develop the next generation of the program, *AlphaGo Lee*. Later, all the insights from many other Go masters were collated into *AlphaGo Master* – which predictably went on to beat *AlphaGo Lee*.

There is an interesting twist to this tale. In 2017 the team at DeepMind wanted to push this further: could a machine beat a human – even if it had not been 'taught' by humans, or had access to training manuals? That is, could it learn from its own behaviours? To test this, the team developed *AlphaGo Zero*. This program played itself repeatedly, knowing only the basic rules of Go, each time testing what moves created a winning formula and over time compiling its own training manual. In total, it took three days of continuous computation time for the program to evolve sufficiently to beat *AlphaGo Lee*, and then a subsequent twenty days to beat *AlphaGo Master*. What intrigued the research team was that after thirty-five days of continuous playing, *AlphaGo Zero* was using game moves that had never been seen before. It was going beyond human play. In doing so it had played the game over 20 million times – possibly about the same number of games, the researchers believed, that had been played by humans in the history of the game.[13]

So it is clear that machines can engage in some tasks that require focus – such chess and Go. And we can predict that over the coming years machines will be developed to perform ever more tasks that require focus. Where does that leave human focus? For if machines can perform *all* tasks of focus, then there is no need to redesign work for human focus.

To understand this better we need to take a closer look at the nature of focused tasks which, it turns out, come in a number of forms. And as you think about the tasks in your company that require focus, it's helpful to distinguish between these different forms. To distinguish these forms of focus and their relationships to the human mind, I use the framework presented in Figure 11.[14]

Along the horizontal axis is the time frame that is being considered – ranging from a second, to a week and through to a year and decade. On the vertical axis (in ascending complexity) are the four types of focus that cognitive tasks require: *correlation* (which considers the extent of the relationship between two or more known variables), *causation* (which applies to cases where a known action causes a known outcome), *imagination* (which imagines novel objects) and

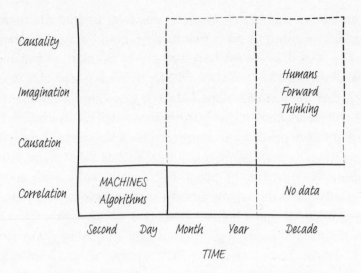

Figure 11. Framework: A typology of ways to focus.

causality (which imagines how these variables – an event, process, state – contribute to the production of another event).

Now as we think about humans and machines, the machines built to beat humans at chess could be located in the lower left quadrant of the framework. These machines are using *algorithms* capable of analysing and correlating vast amounts of known data and performing correlations, which demonstrate the relationship between known data points. The upper quadrants of this model – where the focus is on the future and the task is imagination or causality – are as yet beyond the reach of machines. Machines do not have *imagination* – for example, they cannot imagine another type of game, nor can they approach a situation in terms of *causality* – why relationships between variables exist. It takes a human mind to build hypotheses about why things happen as they do. And in terms of the time dimension, machines cannot think into the future. It takes a human mind to imagine what might be – to think, in other words, into the future. To imagine what might be, not just now, but into the next year, even the next decade. It is these tasks that require human focus.

The value of this capacity to *think forward* is that it brings into the picture aspects that might not yet exist. Machine algorithms deal with what is known – human brains deal with what is unknown and could be.

Think, for example, of a market analyst whose role is already augmented by technology. Analysts have available to them complex analyses of industry data, but in the focused work they are doing they are going beyond the past and the current data to imagine a future time. They are using the available data to create hypotheses about the future. And, importantly, they are calibrating their decisions and making judgements.

Ways to support the power of focus

The power of the human brain to work on tasks that require focus will become ever more important as machines take over the analytical and data-processing segments of work. This process of augmentation puts a renewed emphasis on those practices and processes that support the power of humans to focus. Let's start with the importance of the 'rested brain'.

ACKNOWLEDGE THE CRUCIAL IMPORTANCE OF SLEEP

You might be intrigued by people like the UK Prime Minister Margaret Thatcher, who famously said she got by on four hours' sleep a night. And there are those in high-powered jobs who might have told you they just put in an overnight and are still working this morning. Or you might have experienced yourself getting off an overnight plane journey to go straight into a meeting. Perhaps you felt good about yourself at that moment: you are one of the warrior class and can hold your head up high. But, of course, not everyone functions the same way and working like this over a long period of time is unsustainable.

The science is clear on this. For the human brain to perform the tasks shown in the upper-right quadrant – tasks that require imagination and thinking forward – it has to be rested. Our brains need on average eight hours' sleep in order to be rested and therefore be able to perform those higher human capacities such as imagining or creating hypotheses about causality. So a design question for work is: are there aspects of the way we have designed work that make it tough for people to sleep eight hours a night?

It is not just lack of sleep that messes with our brains, it's also anxiety. When we are anxious, the human brain no longer inhabits the uplands of the thinking and imagining into the future. Instead it reverts right back to the present. It becomes – in other words – more like a machine.

And there is more. When we are pressured and tired, not only are we incapable of forward thinking, we are also unable to perform that valuable human capability – empathy. What is fascinating is that empathy, though emotional rather than cognitive, is also in the top-right corner of the schema. When we empathize with another person we imagine what it is to be them. And our imagination is not confined to what it means to be them now, in the present time. It also imagines what it means to be them in the future. Just as anxiety shuts down forward cognition, it also shuts down forward emotion. It is almost impossible for us to imagine the lives of others when we are so wrapped up in our own lives.

As machines develop, the space for human capability is increasingly about thinking forward and thinking hypothetically. So for those jobs that require focus, having a rested brain will be crucial. You might want to reflect now on the working practices (start time, end time, commute, the 'always on' culture) that make it hard for people to have a good night's sleep. What impact will the new models of work have on this? Some leaders even go as far as to consider that sleep is a strategic resource and encourage a work culture that values sleep, really leverage their wellness programs to improve sleep habits, allow and encourage employees to separate from work when the workday is finished and create nap rooms and encourage their use.[15]

CONFRONT THE MYTH OF MULTITASKING

It's not only teenagers who believe they can simultaneously watch their favourite TV show and work on their school essay. Like working on four hours' sleep, being able to multitask has often been seen as a badge of honour. But human brains are poor at juggling tasks, and when we attempt to do so, we compromise both efficiency and productivity. If we are constantly switching between tasks and being disturbed our attention is broken, we lose the capacity to think either forward or deeply, and we become overloaded and exhausted.[16]

The cognitive friction we experience as a result of multitasking is the opposite of what Mihaly Csikszentmihalyi called 'flow' – feeling in the moment, unaware of the passing of time, completely absorbed in the here and now.[17] The experiences of flow are more likely to happen at times of mental downtime, when you are 'plugged out' rather than plugged in – when you are experiencing peace and quiet.

On the face of it, this should not be difficult to design for. It simply means that work should be designed such that, when people are engaged with focused work, they have blocks of time (minimally two hours) when they are undisturbed. The crucial variable here is time – place is in a sense agnostic. You could have three hours of undisturbed time in the office, at home, in a holiday resort, even perhaps on a long-distance flight.

So why is this, such a seemingly simple design decision, so hard to deliver in practice? Why do countless studies show that most workers are interrupted (or interrupt themselves) on a minute-by-minute basis? And why, given what we know about the impact of exhaustion on the healthy brain – do so many of us have our mobile devices within a hand's reach of our sleeping bodies?

For whilst the challenge of creating focus time is on the surface a scheduling issue, in reality it's much more than that.

SCHEDULE TIME FOR FOCUS

Let's deal with the easy part – scheduling for focus. Those executives who value focus have designed ways to ensure that people, either in the office or at home, have periods of undisturbed time. The impact of this was apparent in one of the most seminal academic studies of work time conducted by Harvard Business School professor Leslie Perlow in the 1990s. She showed how a software engineering team could reduce their feelings of having a 'time famine' and improve productivity by instituting a policy of mandated quiet time, when interruptions were prohibited.[18]

But it turns out that, whilst scheduling for undisturbed time is important, more is required. For whilst we know the benefits of working in an undisturbed way, and are motivated to do so, we inevitably revert to attempts at multitasking. Understanding why we do this and creating a way of working that minimizes its occurrence is crucial.

Let's start by taking a closer look at the first part: why this happens. Ethan Bernstein, Jesse Shore and David Lazer, researchers who together have studied this topic, say there are several obstacles that stand in the way of people voluntarily working alone and focusing.

> For one thing, the fear of being left out of the loop can keep them glued to their enterprise social media. Individuals don't want to be – or appear to be – isolated. For another, knowing what their teammates are doing provides a sense of comfort and security, because people can adjust their own behaviour to be in sync with the group. It's risky to go off on their own to try something new that will probably not be successful right from the start.[19]

That creates the 'always on' default mode so many of us find ourselves slipping into. The pandemic seemed to exacerbate this. For example, IBM data during lockdown showed email traffic increased – particularly in the evening hours between 9 p.m. and midnight.

The result of this always-on mentality is what Brigid Schulte, who directs the Better Life Lab at New America, calls 'time confetti'[20] – the fragmentation of time into all the little bits of seconds and minutes lost to unproductive multitasking. This eats into the time set aside to focus, and often the time set aside for leisure as well. On the face of it, each mundane task takes only a few minutes, but collectively the sheer volume takes time away, and randomly fragments time as a result of numerous interruptions. You will recall periods when you've tried to focus on your task, only to be disturbed by alerts from your team that constantly bring you back to the present. Like homeworkers trying to manage boundaries, each interruption creates a transition that takes time to cognitively recover as it shifts our mind away from focus.[21] So take Christy Johnson's advice and begin by ensuring that teams with a focus task are encouraged to schedule undisturbed blocks of time for each task. She sees this as one of the bedrocks of productivity at Artemis Connection.

Yet it's important to acknowledge that people have different rhythms when it comes to how and where they can focus. For some it will be the first hours of the morning and for others it will be later in the afternoon, so it makes sense to let people take control of blocking out undisturbed time slots. These can be shaped around personal preferences (are they a morning or an afternoon person?), personal circumstances (do they need to look after the kids when they return from school?) or indeed the characteristics of the task (will it take a straight eight hours of undisturbed work to complete?).

ENCOURAGE LEADERS TO ROLE MODEL FOCUS

Fears of being left out of the loop, concerns about being isolated and worry about not being able to be in sync with the group aren't going to simply disappear. So, next, consider the behaviour nudges and cues that will encourage people to switch off. I'm struck by Ethan Bernstein's description of the former CEO of Deloitte US,

Cathy Engelbert. Speaking to a conference, Cathy described realizing the impact of leadership cues when an employee leaving the company (someone she didn't even know) said, 'I didn't want to be like Cathy Engelbert,' working and available to interact with colleagues 'at all hours'.[22] The employee had inferred this – correctly or incorrectly – from repeatedly seeing that Engelbert's instant messaging status was online at night. As Ethan goes on to reflect, 'Unless leaders themselves visibly unplug – meditation rooms and their ilk may become the latest equivalent of the dot-com football table, getting used by people who are the most likely to be laid off during the next downturn.'

Action #8
Reimagine creating focus using asynchronous time

- Take a look back at Action #1 (page 26) to consider those jobs for which a significant number of tasks need focus.
- Consider what needs to be achieved to maximize focus in these jobs. Is the cadence of the job making it hard for people to have eight hours' sleep? Does the scheduling process enable them to have undisturbed blocks of time? If the answer is no, then take a closer look at the ebb and flow of projects.
- Take a look at the ways that encourage people to unplug from work – what examples are leaders setting?
- Acknowledge that because people have their own working rhythms, it is important that, as far as possible, you are able to give them autonomy over when these blocks of time are scheduled.

Reimagine time: Creating coordination with synchronous time

Being disconnected from others and individually focused on the complex task at hand is a central part of some tasks. But for other tasks requiring coordination, those 'in the moment' connections can be crucial. You could be engaged in one-to-one, in the moment coaching with a younger member of the team about your perceptions of how they handled the client meeting. You could be catching up with team members to see how your shared project is going and making last-minute changes to the direction. You could be a member of a senior group pulled together to solve a tough problem that's just arisen and needs to be addressed at speed. You are engaged in a range of coordinating tasks: planning workloads, giving real-time feedback, developing ideas together, setting expectations, sharing information for immediate feedback, managing performance expectations, setting joint goals, building connections, mediating tricky situations.

One aspect to keep in mind about coordination is that it is *place agnostic* – you could be together face to face, but you could also be together on a collaborative platform such as Zoom or Microsoft Teams. So be careful not to assume that all coordination is face to face.

It is also important to realize that more connectivity is *not* always better. That's worth noting in view of the fact that (particularly during the pandemic) people are spending more time with each other at work in some form of coordinated activity. Recall TCS's Ramkumar Chandrasekaran's comments: 'People are spending ridiculously long hours in front of their computers, and the main reason is there are way too many team meetings.' He is not alone in his observation. Studies show that executives spend an average of nearly twenty-three hours per week in meetings. That's up from less than ten hours fifty years ago.[23] The upshot is that the average knowledge worker spends 65 per cent of the work day collaborating and communicating with others (including 28 per cent of the day on email).[24] And the impact of the pandemic is that collaboration has gone omnichannel. These real-time connections could be face to face – in a shared office, a hub, a coffee shop – or virtual, on a platform such as Zoom.

As you redesign work, here are some ways to make the most not only of that precious face-to-face coordination time, but also of virtual coordination.

Make the most of face-to-face coordination

When everyone is in the office most of the time it is possible to muddle through. It's what Cal Newport refers to in his book *Deep Work* as the fuzzy and disorganized process of knowledge work compared to the structured processes of, say, industrial manufacturing. As he observes, 'In many offices, tasks are assigned haphazardly, and there are few systematic ways to track who is working on what or find out how the work is going. In such a chaotic work environment, there are profound advantages to gathering people together in one place.'[25]

Of course, this chaos can have real downsides. I recall talking to my Japanese MBA students and alumni from London Business School about the future of work in this most traditional of countries. One young alumnus, working in a major Japanese bank, had this to say: 'When you are in the office, the manager walks around and gives people work to do. They look to see who might be less busy and ask them to do something. It means I get interrupted a lot.' There are advantages of this looser way of working – but as my Japanese student observed, there is also a great deal more interruption, particularly of junior colleagues.

Yet whilst being face to face can lead to more interruptions, one of the experiences of the pandemic, with face to face minimized, was we got a sense of what was lost. As Microsoft executives discovered from internal surveys, software engineers really missed some aspects of face-to-face group interactions. As one remarked: 'We don't yet have an awesome replacement for getting the right nerds in a room at the same time, with a whiteboard.' They missed planning together, sharing ideas in the moment to change direction and brainstorming.[26] So, getting the most out of face-to-face coordination activities is key.

As working in a shared space such as an office becomes a part of many people's work design, there is a chance to be more intentional about making the most of it. You would be wise to take the advice of Tsedal Neeley, a professor of business administration at Harvard Business School, who blames the modern meeting glut on the assumption that the best way to communicate is verbally.[27] Her advice is that if you do need to meet, then be clear about the communication format. Does everyone need to be present face to face in the same space to exchange information? Would the information be understood best through *lean media* (which is text-based) or *rich media* (which includes non-verbal content)? For example, instant messaging apps are both synchronous (in the sense of simultaneous participation) and lean (primarily text driven) making them ideal for simple coordination, whilst chat – either in person or via video – is both synchronous and rich, so more suited for complex coordination and negotiation. As well as considering the format of the meeting, her advice is to think about who really needs to be there. And specifically to keep meetings as small as possible. Tsedal suggests meetings should be made up of no more than six people to reduce the risk of 'social loafing' when people attend, but don't participate.[28]

Make a virtue out of virtual coordination

As you increase the benefits of face-to-face moments of coordination, in parallel you will need to really boost virtual coordination. There will be many opportunities to do this as the technology of virtual coordination continues through its cycles of innovation. We can get a sense of the momentum of these cycles of innovation by considering the frequency of patent applications using terms associated with remote working, such as 'video conferencing', 'telecommuting', 'remote interactivity' and 'working from home'. In the US such patent applications doubled between January and September of 2020.[29] These patents will be boosted by 'mash-ups' between adjacent technologies – for example the technology company Verizon's acquisition of BlueJeans, a video-conferencing firm; or the acquisition by Adobe of Workfront, a work-management platform for marketers; or Salesforce's acquisition of Slack, a workplace software company. It is clear that many technology firms are pouring every R&D dollar they can into virtual and online technology.

And that will simply accelerate our familiarity with virtual communication and coordination. It was extraordinary how quickly this took off. In February 2000 the Google Meet app use surged so fast that the volumes threatened to exceed the server capacity. Between January and March, Meet's peak daily usage increased thirty-fold, and over the next year people joined more than six billion meetings. Indeed, during one summer peak, users were spending a total of 7.5 billion minutes in Meet every day.

As Sanaz Ahari, who is the senior director of communication products reflected, there was an 'organic adoption of etiquette', particularly tied to the 'hand raise' feature when participants signal a desire to speak. 'There's the beauty of everyone's a tile,' she said. 'Everyone contributes, and there's one way to contribute, whether you're in your living room or whether you're in your office. A tile is a tile is a tile, regardless of your time zone, regardless of your location. And there's something really nice about that from an equitable participation standpoint.'[30]

That's sure to have a real impact on virtual connectivity and it will be crucial to keep updated on this. Take, for example, the developments in virtual reality currently building on Oculus Rift, the technology that PwC used to bring their newly joined graduates together during the summer of 2021. These have the potential to create avatar-type platforms where individuals can walk around, get a sense of the proximity of others, join groups.

These virtual technologies have the potential to become the backbone of virtual coordination. But importantly, simply buying the technology will not be sufficient. As historical studies of the adoption of technology have shown, whilst technological innovation is crucial, to make a genuine difference it has to be accompanied by innovation in organizational and managerial practices and processes.[31] It's the combination of technological innovation *and* working behaviours and practices, such as establishing a rhythm of coordination, that will turbocharge this cycle of productivity.

CREATE A RHYTHM OF COORDINATION

We can expect ever more technological and process innovation around virtual connectivity, but that brings a significant challenge. For as our technological connectivity prowess increases, so too does the attractiveness of always being connected. So as you harness these connectivity innovations, be sure to create practices and processes that enable coordination to be both synchronous – when people are connected – and asynchronous – when people are disconnected. In other words, to create a rhythm of being together and being apart.

The importance of establishing this rhythm was very clear from a series of studies described by Ethan Bernstein.[32] The study considered whether a team, as it engages with a project, also engages with a *rhythm* of coordination – periods of 'sound' when there is connectivity, and periods of 'silence' in the absence of connectivity. To understand this rhythm more rigorously, the research team set up a problem-solving experimental procedure. All the experimental groups were given the same problem to solve, but in some groups team members were always disconnected and isolated, in some groups team members were always connected, and in some groups the team members were intermittently connected. The researchers then measured the performance outcomes of each of these three types of group.

For those groups made up of *disconnected and isolated* members, the strength of the outcomes depended on the strength of the individuals. Theirs was a high-variance set of solutions.

The *always-connected* teams tended to create a rhythm of first pooling their collective information and then using a consensus process to come to a final decision. During their pooling phase they listened to each other, learnt how others were thinking about the solution and debated the options. As a result, when they moved to the consensus phase they inevitably reduced the variance within the information set as they moved to the average solution. That often meant they moved towards a less-than-perfect solution: they gathered information more effectively, but produced less innovative and less productive solutions. Interestingly, as Bernstein observes, 'By achieving more and more connectivity, humans are becoming a bit like passive nodes in a machine network: they are getting better at processing information, but worse at making decisions from it.'

Importantly, it was the group who interacted *intermittently* who became the most innovative and productive. In the first, disconnected phase they were alone and able to think through their own take and perspective on the problem and by doing so come independently to their own unique and often diverse solutions. This was different from the second, always-connected members, who were immediately placed into a group to talk about their ideas. When individuals in this intermittently connected group were subsequently connected with their team members, they had an opportunity to pool their individual solutions and learn from each other. It turns out this process of *collective learning* was crucial. For it showed that even if the individual solutions were not optimal, they might contain a thought or an idea that, if recombined with other solutions, would create a better outcome. In creating collective intelligence, they were accessing the ideas of many, rather than relying on a few individuals with the strongest ideas.

Insight: How TCS creates a rhythm of coordination

This rhythm of connection and intermittent connection will be at the heart of what it takes to create high-performing virtual coordination – and daily and weekly rituals will play a key role.

These coordination rituals began in knowledge-based work more than a decade ago in tasks such as software development. Programmers and managers developed and then deployed an unusually systematic approach to organizing their work. Software firms like Microsoft, IBM and TCS began to employ 'agile' project-management methods. These included 'stand-up' meetings and coding 'sprints' which helped them track and assign tasks without overloading individuals or creating unnecessary interruptions or redundancies.

I took a closer look at how this works in practice at TCS. As the executives Ramkumar Chandrasekaran and Anshoo Kapoor explained to me, they have for some time been operating with location-independent agile working, and it is agile principles that drive the project-management approach. What stood out to me were two synchronous, virtual rituals: the daily stand-ups and the retrospectives.

DAILY STAND-UPS

Daily stand-ups are one of the crucial daily rituals that support virtual coordination at the firm. These take place within small teams, never more than fifteen to twenty people, who come together every day for fifteen minutes. As the executives explain, 'Keeping these meetings short makes them purposeful. They provide an opportunity to talk about what worked yesterday and what didn't. It's also an opportunity to identify the pressing priorities for the day.' In their experience, having data to bring into these conversations is crucial: 'We use live dashboards to track progress. The teams look at where certain work is assigned, the outcome of key deliverables, and whether the project is on schedule or not. The team can see different backlogs and how they are getting delivered. We can look in detail and analyse what went wrong.'

RETROSPECTIVES

Another way to create the rhythm of virtual coordination that TCS have found useful is to mirror the beginnings and ends of projects. They have found it particularly helpful to create 'retrospective' meetings before the team disbands. This is an opportunity for the team to consider how the project went, what they have learnt and the learnings they can take to similar projects. The learnings are boosted by the corporate project data they have access to, which enables them to compare their projects with others. The project leads can then meet virtually with others to understand whether there are any overarching themes that they need to tackle collectively. For example, does the project feedback suggest that new capabilities need to be developed, or that aspects of the project process need to be redesigned?

> *TCS – questions for reflection*
> Does the idea of 'sound' and 'silence' resonate with your rhythms of work? What is your view of the TCS 'daily standups'? Would this bring more connectivity to virtual teams? Would the idea of the 'retrospectives' also build this rhythm?

Coordination – thinking past Mondays and Fridays

During the summer of 2021, in the early days of redesigning work, there was much anxiety about when employees would come to the office. Mark Read, chief executive of advertising firm WPP, voiced what was the concern of many in an interview with the BBC: 'We're never going to go back to working the way we used to work. People are working from home three to four days a week so we probably need 20 per cent less space, but we're not going to do that if everyone's working from home on Mondays and Fridays.'[33]

There are issues here of personal preferences and of what is just and fair. But beyond these is the simple fact that when workers are given complete choice about when to come into the office, most people will naturally gravitate towards working from home two days a week and be in the office three days a week. And their choices of when to be in the office will be the middle of the week, leaving offices empty on Mondays and Fridays.

It seems that whatever the schedule you arrive at, one thing is clear. A significant mistake made in the early automation of work processes was to simply automate the *current* workflow rather than first *redesign* the workflow. As a consequence, too often the process of automation simply replicated the flaws, idiosyncrasies and work-arounds of the current processes. The same is true of the move to face-to-face and virtual coordination. It would be a lost opportunity to simply replicate the assumptions and ways of working currently in place.

In a series of research interviews I have asked executives to describe their perspective on redesigning workflows. An overwhelming view was the importance of simplicity. They said that the more complex the workflow and the scheduling, the less likely employees felt motivated to follow it. And the major tool of simplicity was to remove meetings and team tasks. As executives at TCS told me, 'We constantly ask whether traditional scheduled face-to-face meetings are necessary. Could they be removed and if they are crucial – could they be held asynchronously? We also try to keep coordinated catch-up meetings as short as possible – that's the thinking behind the fifteen-minute daily catch-ups.'

Next, in terms of tasks that have historically required face-to-face coordination, can these tasks be reassigned to people outside the team? Are these tasks that can be performed virtually and asynchronously, giving people back more autonomy over their time? Could they, for example, be performed by freelancers, or indeed alumni of the company?

Insight: How Telstra coordinates with work-scheduling skills

In some companies the role of managing these coordination workflows is considered so crucial that specific roles have been developed to manage them. That's the decision that Alex Badenoch, who leads the people function at the Australian telecoms Telstra, made with the executive team. Alex explained how they went about this:

The company had trained more than 10,000 employees to work in agile teams. We then moved to three levels of management and crucially separated the roles of leader of people and leader of work. The *leader of work* is watching whether the work is humming along. For example, the project demands at any point in time might exceed people capacity, so they have to decide which projects to stop. We are operating dynamically to get the right skill and cost mix. It's important that we don't overcommit people and be mindful of health and well-being.

I asked Alex what she believed was key to getting this right. She made three suggestions. First, she said it's important that people who are managing schedules and resources have accountability and feedback. At Telstra this feedback includes employee engagement, which is measured frequently, a Net Promoter Score, which describes whether an individual would recommend this manager to others, and the retention of team members. Next, it's crucial that scheduling and resource deployment are not simply measured as project outcomes, but also as processes of dynamic capability building. For example, does the way people are assigned to projects and the schedule of their work result in the development of their skills and of project effectiveness? Finally, in Alex's view, one of the keys to making this work is a technical infrastructure capable of creating basic metrics that include resource allocation, skills profiles, work demands and plans of work.

Telstra – questions for reflection

In terms of the rhythm of work, would there be an argument to follow Telstra's example and create a specific 'leader of work'? What is the data you currently have in place to provide feedback on scheduling? Will this be sufficient in the new design of work? Have you in place the 'dynamic building capacity' of Telstra? Is there more you could understand about whether the scheduling is leading to people building their capabilities?

Action #9
Reimagine coordination using synchronous time

- Take a look at the job families and identify those for which coordination is a crucial component. For those coordination tasks, which need to be face to face and which can be virtual?
- For the face-to-face coordination tasks, are there ways you can make these more productive?
- Scrutinize the virtual coordinating tasks. What might be the impact of technological developments? Is there more you could do now to keep abreast of these developments and trial new technologies?
- Take a look at the rhythm of this coordination. Have you got the tempo of connected and unconnected right? Is there more you can do to orchestrate and create daily or weekly rituals?
- Have you created the depth of scheduling capabilities that will be necessary? Is there more that needs to be done?

4. Model and Test

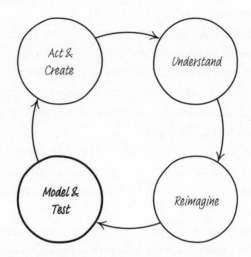

As you redesign work and begin to model how, when and where people will work, you will be faced with many choices and decisions to make. Some ways of working will have clear benefits – others will have trade-offs that you will need to acknowledge and account for. Through the first two steps of this redesign process you've gained insights and a deeper understanding of the elements of work: what supports productivity in your organization, the form of networks and how knowledge flows, and how people within the organization want to work. You've reimagined place and time and considered what it would take to imagine the office as a catalyst for cooperation, the home as a source of energy, asynchronous time as a provider of focus and synchronous time as a creator of coordination. The opportunity now is to bring all of this together and model and then test the redesign of work. My suggestion is there are three factors against which your model should be tested: that it is future-proofed, that it supports technological transitions and that it is capable of being fair and just.

Model and Test: That your redesign is future-proofed
- Framework: A multistage life
- Insight: Verizon, Unilever, Open Banking and CPP Investments
- Action #10

Model and Test: That the model of work supports technology transitions
- Framework: The impact of technology on jobs
- Insight: Australian NSW Public Commission, IBM, TCS and Microsoft
- Action #11

Model and Test: That the model of work is fair and just
- Insight: Brit Insurance and Artemis Connection
- Action #12

Model and Test: That your redesign is future-proofed

For the majority of companies I have supported or observed through the process of redesigning work, a central purpose has been to enable employees to thrive. And because they are designing for the coming years, they have to be sure that their model is future-proofed. To do that you need to have a view of how employees, jobs and technology might change over the short and medium term.

Does your redesign take into account future demographic shifts?

When you consider the type and location of employees, don't imagine that what is occurring now will be static – you need to factor in significant transitions in the average age and size of the population. These transitions are occurring because people are living longer and having fewer children. The simplest way of thinking about this is that the longer people live and the fewer children they have, the older the population becomes and the faster the size of the population declines. Conversely, the longer people live and the more children they have, the larger and younger the population becomes. Let's examine what this means for the 2050 projection of three countries – Japan, China and Nigeria – in order to get a sense of what you might need to take into account.[1]

JAPAN 2050 – AVERAGE AGE FIFTY-THREE, SHRINKING POPULATION

The demographic shift that's taking place in Japan tends to get the headline news – the oldest age at which 50 per cent of the babies born now are expected to live is 107, whilst the country-wide birth rate in 2021 was 1.34 children per family, and 1.13 in Tokyo. Taken together, whilst the average age in Japan in 2020 was forty-six, it will increase to fifty-three by 2050 and the population size will fall from a high of 128 million in 2004, to an expected 109 million by 2050 and 84.5 million by 2100.

CHINA 2050 – AVERAGE AGE FORTY-EIGHT, SHRINKING POPULATION

In China, where increases in life expectancy and decreases in family size have occurred faster than in Japan, in 2020 the average age was thirty-seven. By 2050 this will be forty-eight, and the population, which is currently 1.36 billion, is forecast to fall to 1 billion by 2050.

If we take a look across the world, one in twelve people are currently over the age of sixty-five. By 2050 that will be one in six – that's 450 million people in China, whilst one in five people in Japan will be over eighty. In the United States the number of people aged between sixteen and twenty-four is expected to decline by 10 per cent by 2030, at a time when the baby boomers are moving into retirement.

As you consider these broad global demographic transitions – what impact will they have on the redesign of work? Certainly it means you need to be careful about stereotyping what it is to be over the age of fifty, especially now that people over fifty are becoming a significant part of the population. In the developed countries (like the US and Japan) with shrinking populations, the war for skilled talent will inevitably hot up. As a result the pendulum of power will shift from the employer to the employee, with employees having the upper hand, for example, in their desire for flexibility. Moreover, as the populations shrink in some countries, it would make sense to look to other countries as sources of much needed talent.

Where are the likely sources of much needed talent? It turns out that the story of demographic transitions is not simply one of ageing and population decline. It's also a story of young people and population growth. And that's inevitably creating ever wider differences between countries.

NIGERIA 2050 — AVERAGE AGE TWENTY-TWO, FAST-GROWING POPULATION

Nigeria's demographic profile is an almost mirror image of those in Japan and China. That's because on average people are living longer (and infants are less likely to die), whilst family size remains high, at five children significantly above most of the world. So Nigeria's population, just 38 million in 1950, was by 2021 estimated at 206 million and is projected to be 263 million in 2030 and 401 million in 2050. At that point Nigeria will be the third most populous country in the world. Lagos will be a city of over 24 million – putting it in the top ten of the world's megacities. And, importantly, compared with the ageing populations of Japan and China, in 2021 nearly half the population were under the age of fifteen and only 3 per cent over the age of sixty-five. By 2050 the average age will be twenty-two. When we think about the redesign of work, that's a significant potential pool of young talent.

These demographic transitions raise profound questions for the redesign of work. In countries like Japan and China it will mean enabling people to work into their sixties, seventies and eighties.

In countries like Nigeria the focus will be on educating and providing work for the young. From the perspective of talent pools that means facing up to the realities of likely skill shortages in some countries whilst tapping into the talent pools in others.

Will your redesign help people to thrive in their sixties and beyond?

Here are two tough questions to ask of the design of work model: are you stereotyping what it is to age and be productive, and by doing so closing opportunities to those over sixty? And, in the redesign of work, are you focusing too much on the needs and aspirations of those in their twenties and thirties, whilst discounting the over-fifties?

Often our view of how people age imagines rapid physical and cognitive decline. Yet, as my colleague Andrew Scott has shown, the lengthening of life is about more productive, healthy years.[2] For whilst the period of morbidity (when you are ill before you die) has not decreased, it takes proportionally less of the total span of life as longevity increases. The result is that, when life extends, productive years increase.

Moreover, with the passage of time comes the opportunity to develop *crystalline intelligence*. This is the accumulated insights, networks, knowledge, wisdom and strategies that are built over time. It differs from *fluid intelligence*, which encompasses information processing, memory use and deductive reasoning. Over a lifetime there seems to be a constant fluctuation in the relative strengths of these different mental skills.

In our late teens we may be fast at calculating numbers and working out patterns; in our thirties our short-term memory may peak; in our forties and fifties our social understanding is at its highest. Harvard Medical School's Laura Germine and Boston College's Joshua Hartshorne put it this way: 'At any given age, you're getting better at some things, you're getting worse at some other things, and you're at a peak at some other things. There's probably not one age at which you're peak on most things, much less on all of them.'[3]

Perhaps it's no surprise therefore that some companies have found, when it comes to the design of work, that a combination of the young and old can be the most productive. Moreover, older workers can play a significant role in sharing their crystalline intelligence, their wisdom and know-how. That's going to be particularly crucial in sectors where there will be a shortage of skilled young people.

Insight: How Verizon supports older employees with 'legacy skills'

A skills shortage was the challenge for the US telecoms company Verizon. Its field-based technicians are required to support both new technologies such as fibre and legacy technologies such as copper-wire connections. These older systems will decline in use, but there will still be a lengthy transition period before they become completely obsolete.

Michael Sunderman, Verizon's director of global learning and development, explained to me how they approached making the best use of 'legacy skills'. The company has designed work so as to identify and connect older employees who were experts in these legacy technologies. Some were currently employed, others retired. These legacy experts were brought into projects to provide vital support and coaching to field-based technicians when they encountered problems with unfamiliar older systems.

This support took a number of forms. In some cases the experts worked with the technicians in the field, but not all field-based engineers had a local expert at hand, so even before the pandemic, the link between the two was often virtual. Whilst normal virtual communication such as phone calls, emails and messaging played a role, for some situations the expert needed to see what the field engineer was looking at. Michael explained that he and his team partnered with a number of augmented-reality technology companies to develop new equipment and software tools that would supplement these conversations by collecting a range of visual data. To do that some field technicians were equipped with augmented-reality goggles that enabled their office-based expert coaches to share and analyse what the technician in the field could see and talk them through solutions in real time.

> **Verizon – questions for reflection**
> What will be the age profile of your employees in five, ten, fifteen years? As you look at the jobs now and in the future are there any that require 'legacy skills'? Do you know where these jobs are? Will this model of work motivate and retain legacy-skilled employees?

Does your redesign prepare for the future importance of a multistage life?

Longer lives are not simply creating design issues for the old – they are also increasingly impacting on the choices that people will take to thrive right across their working lives.

That's because as we live longer, the ebb and flow of our working life naturally morphs. The sequence of the traditional three stages of full-time education, full-time work and full-time retirement becomes a lifetime sequence that is more akin to multistages illustrated in Figure 12. Fundamentally, this is a great deal more flexible and idiosyncratic.

Unrestricted by the constraints of three stages, additional stages will naturally emerge and the lifetime sequence of work assumes a more free-flowing path. The challenge, and indeed the marvel of a multistage life is that there are so many possible paths to take – each stage is no longer occupied by a single age cohort. You could be twenty-five and taking time out to explore the world – but you could also be forty-five or sixty-five. And again, you could be twenty-five and enrolled in an educational institution – but you could also be thirty or fifty.

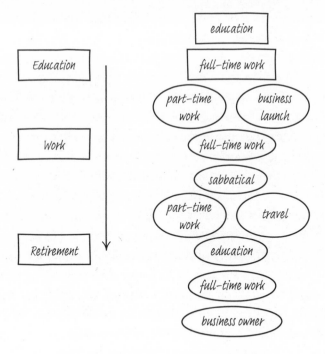

Figure 12. Framework: A multistage life.

These multistage freer-flowing life paths inevitably have more transitions between their various phases. A traditional three-stage life path had only two transitions – between education and work and between work and retirement. And, importantly, these stages were taken in lockstep with others of roughly the same age: teenage or early twenties for the transition from education to work, and mid sixties for the transition from work to retirement. When people are in lockstep with others, there is little reason to cultivate personal agency or self-insight. It's possible to simply look around at what others are doing and follow their lead.

As more people transition to multistage lives so they will inevitably have greater personal agency. By making these types of choice about their life path, they will inevitably become more proficient and self-directed about other aspects of their working life. What might start with 'social pioneers', for example the few over-sixties who start their own business or travel around the world, becomes more widespread and unexceptional.

Might talented people want to join your company at a number of possible times in their multistage working life rather than only as graduates? And when they are working with you, are you reducing flexibility by insisting that they have to work as a full-time employee? Are you considering creating more flexible arrangements that would enable your most talented people to build a portfolio of working activities that might include founding their own business, working in a not-for-profit or learning a new skill?

As working lives inevitably transform from three-stage to multi-stage, how do your models of work acknowledge and support people's changing hopes and aspirations? Let's take a closer look at how the executive teams at Unilever, Open Banking and CPP Investments went about building a way of working that acknowledged that, for some people, the ability to be flexible about how they worked would be both helpful and attractive.

Insight: How Unilever created a future-proofed 'third-way'

It was questions of flexibility Morag Lynagh and Placid Jover from Unilever began to work on from 2017. Morag is the firm's global future-of-work director whilst Placid is vice-president of human resources across Latin America and leads the company's New Employment Models agenda globally. Together they decided that they wanted to create what they called a 'third way'. As Placid explained to me from Montevideo, 'In response to a world that was inflexible, our dream was to increase access to in-demand skills and bring greater flexibility to our resourcing options. To do that we wanted to engage and retain people longer.'

FLEXIBILITY ACROSS THE LIFE CYCLE

Part of their focus was on life-cycle events. An obvious group was the over-fifty-fives. As Morag explained, 'It doesn't feel right at the age of fifty-five or sixty to ask someone to sit on the bench. We really need their insights and wisdom.' However, their data analytics showed that this flexibility wasn't just important to the older generation, it was also important to others. In fact, they realized that people at *any* stage of life can value flexibility. As Placid described:

> We realized that flexibility was valuable to people for many reasons. Take for example the young graduate who wants to be associated with the company but is also really motivated to create an income stream that enables them to explore the world. Or the person in their thirties who wants to build their own business as a side-hustle. Or someone who wants to work with us, but also wants to learn from a smaller, specialist organization.

In thinking about the personas of these types of people, they realized that the unlocks to these various needs would be both flexibility and personalization. Placid again:

> The bottom line was that we needed to create a new type of employment contract – to create a 'third way' which at that time did not exist. We wanted to fill the white space between being a full-time employee and being a contractor or agency worker from a third-party organization. We wanted to move from 'owning' talent to 'accessing' talent, and new employment models allow us to do this.

THE U-WORK MODEL

So, in the UK they began to pilot what this could look like. They spotted the opportunity to open up and create more personalized employment options so employees could move from working fifty-two weeks a year, to taking on projects that fitted into the rhythm of their lives. In this model, called U-Work, employees receive a monthly retainer and earn assignment pay. Importantly, a key part of this flexible employment model is the provision of pension support, access to healthcare insurance and the opportunity to engage with Unilever's ongoing online learning resources.

Morag and Placid described how U-Work actually played out in the lives of three Unilever employees: Adam, Roy and Susanna.

Adam had recently completed Unilever's Future Leaders programme in supply chain and wanted to combine work with travel. He signed up for U-Work and joined the global ice-cream supply-chain group to support the director for a six-month full-time project. In this role he focused on the feasibility of a new project and created a stakeholder map. This design of work brought the flexibility that Adam wanted; it also worked well for the director, who didn't want a permanent employee but needed to add skill and know-how quickly. The real benefit over using an outside free-lancer was that Adam knew Unilever, knew the culture, had the vital internal networks and could hit the ground running.

Roy was a manufacturing manager with more than forty-five years' experience at Unilever. He was not ready for full-time retirement and his manager worried that his expertise could be lost to the company. So he became a performance mentor for the business leaders, on site for two days a week, for two months.

Susanna, a trained lawyer, wanted a portfolio life that included caring for her children and a part-time role with a media-law firm. So, she combined working with the Unilever law group on a mixture of projects with providing legal guidance to a start-up media-law business. The benefit for Susanna was that she was able to pick up a project immediately and seamlessly whilst developing her skills in a new area (media law). Her Unilever manager benefited from having someone who was trustworthy and who knew the business and – importantly for Susanna – there was no need for a job estimate or a purchase order.

By the first quarter of 2021 U-Work was up and running in the UK, Mexico, Argentina and the Philippines, and had been taken up by a wide demographic of people for all sorts of reasons. The feedback from line managers was that they could source people with crucial skills very quickly. And interestingly, of those people who joined U-Work, none had decided to return to their previous employment contract.

In the summer of 2021 I asked Morag and Placid how the model was going and what they had learnt. They called out a number of important takeaways, especially with more markets now coming on board. First, they discovered that many people who choose this way of working tend to be those who are skilled at networking and have built a strong, credible reputation. Second, as the initiative developed, Morag and Placid realized they needed to create a new role – the 'contact manager' – to be ambassadors of the model and support the U-Workers by making connections between what managers need and what employees can provide. Next, this flex model works best where work can be broken into individual projects and assignments that the U-Worker can pick up with ease. And lastly, it's not for everyone – their calculation is that between 2 and 4 per cent of the workforce will be interested in this option. But with around 150,000 employees, that's still a significant group of about 4,000.

Morag and Placid are now looking wider at other 'third-way' employment models. As they say, 'Once we have cracked the code we can widen. We are now thinking about how we can support students and the wider population, how to support people on paid learning sabbaticals. This is a real opportunity to be creative about the redesign of the employment contract.'

Unilever – questions for reflection
As you look at the current and future demography of your workforce, is there evidence that more of your talented and valuable people will want flexibility? Does the model of work factor this in with regard to flex options, and, with this in mind, would a model like the U-Work model at Unilever be appropriate?

Insight: How Open Banking prepares for the future with job-sharing

Building employment contracts that create a 'third way' has been part of the creative challenge for the team at Unilever. Another way of imagining this is to consider keeping a permanent role but sharing it between two people, who together create a way of working that meets the continuity needs of clients and projects. Role sharing in this manner makes particular sense in posts that are more difficult to fill, that need continuity, and that cannot easily be separated into standalone projects performed by a part-time worker or indeed a U-Worker.

Job-sharing was the job model that Sherelle Folkes and Nichola Johnson-Marshall adopted in the financial company Open Banking. Open Banking creates software standards and industry guidelines to drive competition, innovation and transparency in UK retail banking.[4] Initially, Nichola was a part-time contractor working on external communications. When the job scaled up the executive team decided to create the option of role sharing and hired Sherelle, who joined as co-head of external communications.

The flexibility this brought was important to both: Nichola could build a boutique consultancy; Sherelle could write a book. As Sherelle says, 'We are definitely the upbeat communications team of Open Banking because you're getting that work–life balance. How many people end up having to leave a job to take a career break or a sabbatical because they're burning out?' They also discovered that, rather than bringing one person's experience, network and mindset to the challenges of the job, they brought two perspectives. As Sherelle says:

> You can learn from each other, quite often there are things that Nichola will pick up and certain things that she'll do, and it makes it better. And I actually think, 'Oh, that's an extra thing I didn't think of.' So certainly for a firm, you're going to get double the talent, double the capability, double the experience.

A POSITIVE IMPACT ON PRODUCTIVITY

There is a growing body of evidence that sharing a role has a positive impact on productivity and well-being. And whilst it takes time for any job-share to get into a groove, it can accomplish more in the long term. A UK study estimates that people participating in role sharing are 30 per cent more productive compared with traditional roles.[5] Data from the UK Civil Service – which has around 1,000 role sharers within its workforce of over 300,000 – also found that job-shares reported 11 per cent higher well-being (higher than any other group including part-time, full-time and contractors).[6]

What might be the basis of this productivity gain? This was a question I put to Sophie Smallwood and Dave Smallwood who are co-CEOs of the technology platform Roleshare, which matches professionals to co-apply for jobs. As they told me:

> Certainly having different skills and networks and the ability to have headspace away from work is a real boost. But there is also a productivity boost from the amount of learning that happens in the pair. It's like having a built-in coach and there is healthy peer pressure because you know you are handing the work off to someone else. To use an athletics metaphor – they are racing to hand over the baton and they want to put in their best performance. Plus, they don't have the midweek dip that full-time workers can have. They are super focused on the three days. It's more than an employment contract – it's a social contract and you simply don't want to drop the baton and let the other person down.

Open Banking – questions for reflection
Are there any examples of job-sharing currently in your business? What have been the lessons learnt? Would this be appropriate to extend more widely? And if there are no examples, would this be an interesting pilot to experiment with?

Insight: Why CPP Investments enables people to 'work for three months from anywhere'

Recall that at CPP Investments, as Dario Kosarac explained to me, 'the investment horizon is the next quarter century', and this long-term focus is implicit in the attitude to the redesign of work. 'We are pursuing the "golden model". We don't want to be a place that exploits and burns people out. We want to keep our colleagues engaged, motivated and balanced.'

They are particularly interested in those people who are highly talented and value flexibility (the bottom-right quadrant in Figure 5). Let's take a closer look at how they went about pursuing this 'golden model'. Before the pandemic the senior team were building a model of work with a message that 'you are here for the long term'. This long-term focus was an echo of the purpose of the fund management strategy. As Dario puts it, 'We are not here to make a group of people rich, we're investing the funds of over twenty million Canadians and helping to provide a retirement security.'

Building human capabilities and engagement for the long term mirrored this corporate purpose. To build long-term engagement, the team had already experimented – for example with a sabbatical programme that gave people with five years' experience the option to take at least three months off from work to pursue other passions or interests, whether that be learning a new language or spending time with family. They could also request up to a year of unpaid leave. This has been important, as Dario reflects:

> Our people really are driven and they are working hard, dedicating a lot of their time to work. We don't want them to burn out and feel the only way out is to quit. We want to provide colleagues with a means to take a break in their career or time away from work activities. It's important to provide the opportunity to be well-rounded citizens and, if they so choose, find other ways to engage with the world.

As the pandemic progressed, the senior team had a chance to learn and innovate around other aspects of the design of work. My advisory group HSM Advisory supported the design team in some of these activities. Like many multinational companies, in lockdown a proportion of their employees were trapped in a jurisdiction far from their office of employment. One person, for example, had been visiting their family in Korea and travel restrictions meant they could not travel back. In the light of these experiences, the company's mobility team began to ask, 'If you are a foreign national and you happen to be visiting your family, is it OK for you to work remotely while still maintaining corporate compliance and risk-mitigation requirements? How do we ensure business continuity?' As Dario reflected, 'When we looked back on 2020 and 2021 we had very good returns; we'd closed important deals; we'd been able to still actively look for investment opportunities, from buying bridges to trading public securities.' Amidst the pandemic, the fund reported its highest ever annual returns of 20.4 per cent.

To understand what was possible, Dario and his colleagues put together a cross-functional design team including mobility experts, tax advisors and legal experts. Very quickly they honed in on crucial aspects of the success of the firm during the pandemic – the firm's investment in technology platforms and the characteristics of many CPP roles.

In terms of the four productivity elements described earlier, productivity in many of the core CPP Investment positions is about focus and coordination: focus in terms of individual thinking, analysing and writing; coordination in terms of working with others on ideation and exchange. And as the team had learnt during the pandemic, with the right communication tools it was possible to mimic most of this remotely. This capacity was boosted by the company's significant investments in cloud-based technological platforms such as SharePoint, which, prior to the pandemic, had enabled employees to be connected and access systems in an efficient, quick and secure way. Importantly, these secure platforms also enabled remote employees to access the highly commercially sensitive material crucial to their work.

So the pandemic, with people working at home, sometimes thousands of miles away from their office, gave the design team a chance to assess what was possible. One important learning was that, for those jobs that required focus, being out of a busy office was a boost to productivity. As Dario reflects:

> We discovered there are productivity losses when people are in the office with colleagues coming by their desk every two minutes saying, 'Hey, can we do this?' Or, 'What do you think of that?'

Being remote had benefits if the individual was able to manage their environment bespoke to them, in a way that minimized distractions.

As the design team studied the engagement and productivity data they realized that, as long as people could focus and use the technology platforms to coordinate, then place was less important. Their thinking was that if someone can perform their work from home, then logically they can work from anywhere. So they began to play around with the idea that people would have the opportunity to work anywhere for three months.

This was not a straightforward model – issues arose around immigration, corporate and personal tax and how benefits (in the event of illness or death, for example) worked in these circumstances. The challenge CPP faced was how to create these options without triggering risk and compliance issues. So the design team set about talking with the top executive team about possible terms of engagement, the likely impact on retention and the possible trade-offs.

They began to model the options, looking in detail at various location configurations and identifying what they called 'jurisdictional pairs'. For example, if an individual is employed in one country office, what other jurisdictions might have relatively clear rules so that risks and complexity could be managed to accommodate location flexibility? These they called 'phase one' countries, of which there are about twenty with different jurisdictional permutations. The design team then went on to identify 'phase two' countries, which included places that are creating the Nomad visa, which is a facilitated way for non-citizens to be able to work remotely from those countries.

ALIGNMENT WITH CORPORATE PURPOSE

For the team at CPP Investments, the importance of linking these flexible practices to the purpose of the company was clear. This gave it real momentum, because it aligned with the purpose of the company to invest in the long term. For example, enabling people to work anywhere for three months a year would be a real distraction in a company where people are only expected to stay a few years, but if they are going to be there for longer then, as Dario told me, 'Across the span of a whole career, this is a very small part of their working life with us.' The design team also learnt, as the team at Unilever had, that the implementation of these flexible options can be complex and require specialist skills to design, which at CPP Investments meant consulting tax, technology and mobility experts.

I asked Oliver Ferriman, who led the CPP project for my advisory group HSM Advisory, what we had learnt. He made three points:

First, it is clear that 'the time is now' – the sheer demand for flex from employees was significant. Second, we saw that culture is key, and this was an opportunity to really dial up trust and agility. Third, we saw that everyone is accountable – understanding the importance of distributed accountability and signalling that everyone at the firm is learning and experimenting together, rather than the responsibility sitting with leadership. People approached the design survey and workshops with a sense of reciprocal responsibility, overwhelmingly acknowledging that this flex model was a two-way deal, with individuals and teams responsible for making it work.

CPP Investments – questions for reflection
How many of your high-value people have family or homes outside the place they work? Is this a significant number? If it is significant, would giving them an opportunity to live in another country or have a sabbatical be motivating? As you think about how best to go about making this happen, consider who would need to be involved and the complexities you are likely to face.

Action #10
Model and Test that the model is future-proofed

- Does the model of work take into consideration that there are likely to be more people over fifty in the workforce? Have you ensured that the crystalline intelligence of older workers is factored into the design of work?
- Have you factored in that people are living multistage lives? Have you been too rigid about the points of entry into the company and should you redesign work in a way that is more project-based to enable this employment flexibility?
- What will be the short and medium term impacts of the demographics of the countries your businesses are and will be operating in? Are there places where population decline will lead to a skill shortage? Consider how best to factor this into the design of work and whether you need to think more creatively about other pools of talent.
- Take a look at the process you have to support flexibility such as different employment models, job-sharing, sabbaticals and time working in another location. Consider whether these would fit with your corporate

purpose and the strategy you have for engaging and retaining talented people.

Model and Test: That the model of work supports technology transitions

One of the astounding effects of the pandemic was the acceleration of digital skills and the extent to which it fast forwarded the adoption of a wide range of new technologies. In the context of automation and the role of machines, whilst there will be major accelerations in this area in cognitive work, ultimately machine usage will be focused on algorithms and correlations. Machines will not focus on the long-term human imagination that will be crucial to some work. Yet even with this limited use, as we saw in Chapter 2: Understand, the impact of technological development is sure to shape what people want from work. In the face of this acceleration in automation, people will inevitably be anxious about losing their jobs, and motivated to either upskill in their own job or even reskill to a new one.

It is inevitable that your redesign of work will encompass many digital and automated elements. So, as you go about modelling and testing your model, the extent to which it can make the most of these technological transitions will be a factor to consider. Here we begin by looking at the employee experience of job automation and how pathways of automation are described. Next, we consider more general models of the impact of machines on work and then take a closer look at developing those aspects of skills that machines cannot engage with – human skills such as empathy and judgement. Finally, we look more closely at the corporate initiatives that are supporting this skill development and transition.

How employees experience job automation

Most employees know that automation will have a profound impact on their work. Indeed, as Peter Brown, who leads the HR group at

PwC in the UK, shared with me in March 2021, the PwC general-worker survey reported that 40 per cent of respondents thought their job would be obsolete in five years. At the same time, 40 per cent said they'd been digitally upskilled in the last year and 80 per cent were confident they could adapt to this new world. That feeling of personal agency and mastery is great for the executive team at PwC, but not all employees feel the same. Other surveys suggest more than 60 per cent of workers worry about their job becoming obsolete and that they won't have the skills to adapt.[7]

Both these aspects of personal agency and of potential anxiety could play a defining role in whether your model of the redesign of work lands with employees. Taking a look across the whole population of jobs, it's been calculated that, for 60 per cent of jobs, one in three tasks can be automated. For many employees that's a substantial change in the nature of their work.[8]

You want to redesign work so that people are able to thrive, and we know that people thrive when they feel confident about their capacity to adapt to this new world, and specifically confident that they can work with machines. They believe that if part of their job were to be automated, they could *upskill* to perform the more complex tasks of their job that remained, or *reskill* to a completely different job. People who feel anxious about the speed and trajectory of automation will find it much harder to learn and adapt.

In order to be upbeat and confident about the redesign of work, employees need to know the likely pathways of automation for their own jobs. They also need to feel confident they will have the opportunity and ability to build the new capabilities these pathways of automation reveal.

That's why some executive teams have put resources behind analysing and understanding these pathways of automation and then communicating these to employees so they can develop strategies to guide their actions. The government of one Australian state is a case in point.

Insight: How the New South Wales Public Commission
understands the pathways of automation

As Chris Lamb, who is the deputy commissioner for the New South Wales Public Commission, told me, understanding how jobs will change over the next decade and supporting employees through these potential pathways was a major focus of activity for the commission. Employing around 400,000 people across the state in jobs that include transportation, education and healthcare, the commission provides work for around 10 per cent of the total workforce in the state. That means it also has a significant impact on communities.

To create a deeper understanding of how jobs would change, from 2019 the commission partnered with a specialist data-analytical group to take a deep dive into the data about tasks and skills. As Chris explained:

> We knew that it would be important to understand how the existing workforce would change over the next ten years. We looked at the level of tasks and skills and wanted to know which jobs would be automated, which augmented and where new jobs would be added. We also wanted to understand to what extent jobs could be performed remotely. That is because as a government we want to focus on the whole region and not simply the major cities such as Sydney, Wollongong and Newcastle.

Using a range of probability analytics, the team predicted that of the 400,000 jobs, around 42,000 would be augmented and 15,000 would be completely automated, whilst another 9,500 jobs would be created – largely for skilled data scientists.

As the future job analytics data became clearer they were shared with the various government departments. This gave each department an opportunity to drill down on their own data sets and to use these insights to support long-term planning and resource allocation.

MODELLING NEW WAYS OF WORKING

Understanding how jobs would change over the next decade enabled departments to test their current workforce models against these predictions. Some took this as an opportunity to make bold strategic choices about the design of work. For the executive team at the Department of Transport there was already a shared awareness that driverless trains and trucks would have a significant impact on transport services across the state. As they put together the predicted future pathways of automation and the likely impact on future skills, they discovered significant skill similarities across the state's three major transport systems – rail, bus and ferry services.

These analytical insights allowed the department's executive team to make a number of bold strategic decisions in their models of the future workforce and ways of working. They decided that, rather than continue with the three traditional lines of business (rail, bus and ferry) they would realign the future work structure and skills around the customer experience and the customer journey.

The insights from the data analytics enabled the executive team to then embark on a series of workshops and conversations with employees about how their work was changing, how it was likely to change in the future, and the learning provisions that would be created to guide them. From this initial data analysis a whole series of pilots were initiated to support employees through the work-change journey. For example, one of the design teams created a partnership with an external learning company skilled in developing learning experience platforms. Together they were able to use the analytics from the job data about the most valuable future skills to be sure that learning resources were directed in the right way. As Chris told me:

> We piloted with 500 employees and found that many were going to Google if they wanted to learn something. Because our learning

platform sits on Google Chrome we were able to nudge employees towards our own learning materials rather than generic materials on YouTube. That meant we could build a stronger learning community who were accessing similar materials.

The design team also began to pilot a raft of initiatives around boosting the crucially important digital skills. They'd learnt from the initial job analytics that many of the augmented roles needed digital capabilities, whilst many of the new jobs would have a significant digital element. So another set of pilots considered how best to build these valuable and hard-to-come-by digital skills.

The team began by developing a capability framework for data scientists and then fashioned a new career path that began as people joined as graduates. They also looked closely at retention strategies. As Chris remarked, 'We know that the challenge is keeping data scientists who are often quickly poached by the consulting practices once they have developed their capabilities. So, we have to strengthen within the organization a good reason to stay.' There are two areas of importance that Chris and his team have identified:

> The government is dealing with some of the most complex and biggest problems in the country – so we want to ensure people realize this and are really excited by these possibilities. But it's more than this. A lot of people join the government because of a sense of purpose and service to the community – so we want to ensure that we continue to build that sense of purpose and community as we go about redesigning work.

STRENGTHENING COMMUNITIES

One of the ways the commission is reinforcing this sense of purpose is to use the potential of homeworking to strengthen neighbourhoods and communities outside of the major cities. As Chris remarked:

Our data analytics had shown there were jobs that could on paper be done outside of the office. What our collective experience of Covid had taught us was that this could actually be possible. People had made the mindset shift to working from home. The approach we've taken is to position head office jobs as location agnostic. That doesn't mean, by the way, that people can live in Barbados or Fiji. As a public service it's important our employees are part of the community they serve and are paying taxes in the state. We wanted to use this as an opportunity to continue our mission to invest in regional cities such as Bathurst and Orange, some of which are over 500 miles from Sydney. And it was important that it was not just administration jobs that moved – we also wanted leadership roles to move to the region. We see this as a real opportunity to strengthen neighbourhoods – when a regional town has a base of government employees it attracts talent and local businesses prosper – we see this as an enabling factor.

NSW Commission – questions for reflection
Consider how much you already know about the pathways of automation in the key jobs in your business. Would it be worthwhile, as the NSW Public Commission has done, to invest in the analytics to take a closer look at this? If you do have these analytics, are you using them to test the model of work against them?

Framing the impact of automation on jobs

As you model and test the redesign of work, you'll need, like Chris Lamb and his team, to factor in the impact of machines on work. MIT economist David Autor, who co-leads the MIT Work of the Future research institute,[9] developed the schema shown in Figure 13.

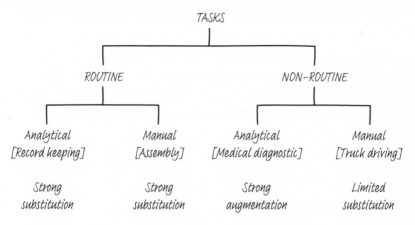

Figure 13. Framework: Predicting the impact of machines on work.

Here is what the schema shows. It starts by analysing jobs at the level of their component *tasks* (recall from Chapter 2 that for most jobs there are about thirty tasks). Next, the schema considers these tasks in terms of the degree to which they are routine or non-routine. Highly *routine* tasks are those that can be easily written down in a manual, performed by following instructions, and always performed in a similar way. The jobs of the call-centre workers at BT are examples of highly routinized tasks. In terms of their knowledge component, such tasks tend to have a great deal of *explicit knowledge* associated with them.

Non-routine tasks are a great deal more complex and can be different every time. Some of the tasks in the analytical jobs at CPP Investments are non-routine in the sense that when the likely revenue pathways of a major investment are modelled, the outcomes across companies will be different and therefore have to be judged separately. These types of task tend to have a high component of *implicit knowledge* associated with them.

As the schema shows, these routine and non-routine tasks can be further divided by the extent to which they are *analytical* or *manual*. Analytical tasks are those that require cognitive functioning such as problem solving or analysis of data; manual tasks require some form of physical activity.

It was this type of modelling that the design team at the NSW Commission used to predict the likely pathways of automation. Let's take a closer look at each of the four possible outcomes and the predicated pathways of automation.

ROUTINE / ANALYTICAL – STRONG SUBSTITUTION

In many routine tasks, machines (both AI and robots) can and in some cases have already substituted for humans. That's the case for analytical tasks such as record keeping, calculations and repetitive customer services.

ROUTINE / MANUAL TASKS – STRONG SUBSTITUTION

The substitution of machines for humans is also substantial in manual tasks such as picking and sorting or repetitive assembly tasks. Yet whilst machines can perform some of these manual tasks, there are many they can't as yet. That's because, despite advances, robots simply don't have the flexibility and dexterity of human workers. Like all machines, robots learn from data and repetition, which makes them remarkably adept at a certain task, but only that one. As an MIT report on automation explained, a fine-tuned gripping robot can pluck a glazed doughnut and carefully place it in a box, with its shiny glaze undisturbed, but that gripper only works on doughnuts, it can't pick up a clump of asparagus or a car tyre.[10]

Moreover, these machines are costly, so have tended to be deployed in countries of high-cost labour (such as South Korea and Japan), or where the job is particularly complex and skilled. Inevitably, this cost and the operational expertise required will slow the widespread adoption of robots.

NON-ROUTINE / ANALYTICAL – STRONG AUGMENTATION

The impact of machines on non-routine tasks is an area of immense interest. For non-routine analytical tasks, such as forming hypotheses, medical diagnostics and persuading and selling, it is the *combination* of human and machine that is creating strong augmentation. Here human skills are augmented by machine data, analogues and information. In jobs at CPP Investments those engaged in the business case analysis are making use of sophisticated automated modelling to provide base data. As in many jobs, these are activities where humans and machines are working together. In Chapter 5 we will take a closer look at how IBM is augmenting the work of managers by supporting them through the design and deployment of a range of bots programmed to provide timely behavioural nudges. The machine reminds the manager, for example, that it's time to talk with a team member, or will provide in-the-moment guidance through a check-list of how best to perform this task.

NON-ROUTINE/MANUAL – LIMITED SUBSTITUTION

These are tasks such as janitorial services or truck driving which could be impacted by, for example, robot floor cleaners or driverless trucks. But this is still relatively limited substitution because there are a host of activities like navigating staircases or congested town centres that are proving hard for machines.

As the MIT report states, 'Technology has always replaced some jobs, created new ones and changed others. The question is whether things will be different this time as robots and artificial intelligence quickly take over for humans on factory floors and in offices.'[11] They concluded that change would be more evolutionary than revolutionary. That perspective is important as you go about redesigning work. What might this evolution look like? 'We anticipate that in the next two decades, industrialized countries will have more job openings than workers to fill them.' That's the sort of skill shortage that could easily derail your model of the redesign of work. Work can only be redesigned if there are employees who are motivated and able to perform this work. How might you ensure this happens?

Part of it, as the NSW team discovered, is to motivate employees to upskill by providing insights about how their job will morph and where the new tasks will emerge. Importantly, this insight also cautions employees against allocating resources to upskill into tasks that have a high probability of being automated.

As a humanistic psychologist, I start from the position that most adults (whatever their pay grade) are motivated to learn and develop skills in order to build resilience against current challenges and guard against future shocks. They do this by investing time and resources (sometimes significant amounts of both) to upskill in their current job – or, better still, they reskill in the hope and anticipation of securing a better, higher-value job. As Matt Sigelman, CEO of the labour market platform Burning Glass Technologies, remarked to me, 'People have an irrepressible desire and ability to move up.'

This human drive will turn out to be crucial in the face of the massive job churn ahead. So, the real motivational kicker in the redesign of work is to create a learning infrastructure that enables and encourages employees to harness this innate human drive. To do so, I've seen executives build foundational human skills, make the developmental pathways visible so that employees know how to connect to better and often higher-paid work, and support mobility by investing in skill development opportunities not only for current employees, but for the wider supply chains and communities as well.

The challenge of building foundational human skills

What human skills will be most valuable as we look to the future? We know that, right now and in the foreseeable future, machines are generally poor at understanding a person's mood, at sensing the situation around them and at developing trusting relationships. So, as the World Economic Forum report on the future of jobs suggested, it is foundational human skills such as empathy, context sensing, collaboration and creative thinking that will be vital.[12]

The focus on foundational human skills was clear in retail bank branches as ATMs dispensed cash and online banking provided bank statements. This automation freed up time for the bank staff to be upskilled to become more active ambassadors, cross-selling to customers and suggesting other bank products. Importantly, this 'human' part of the job required high levels of interpersonal skills such as empathy, listening and judgement.

Yet in terms of upskilling, developing these foundational human skills is far from easy. The paradox is that, whilst there is understanding about how to develop the cognitive skills of analysis, decision-making and analytical judgement, a great deal less is known about the genesis of foundational human skills. Indeed, much of the context of how people learn and perform is currently skewed towards cognitive skills. This is an issue that has been on my mind for more than a decade, and in my view there are three hurdles to the development of foundational human skills that have to be overcome: the education process at schools, how technology is used in the home and the extent of stress at work.[13] There is probably little you can do about the education process and home environment – but there could be much you could do about stress at work.

THE EDUCATION PROCESS

Most schools are simply too much like factories, and still reflect the basic foundations of education laid down after the Industrial Revolution. The aim by the early 1900s was clear: to take a population that was mainly engaged in craft or agricultural work and prepare it for work in factories – and, more recently, offices. Though some schools now teach some foundational human skills, in many schools these traditions hold firm: children are trained to stay still for hours at a time (as they would on a factory production line), to engage in rote learning, and to be compliant and follow rules. The pity is that these skills are the very ones at which machines are highly competent.

These conditions do little to nurture the skills of compassion, inventiveness, or the ability to interpret people's emotions correctly. Of course, the reconfiguration of the educational system will not be on your agenda for redesigning work, although there are a host of new educational institutions that are attempting to put these foundational human skills centre stage. You should, however, be aware that when young people join your organization they may well lack the sophistication of human foundational skills that will be crucial to their future success and might well need specific upskilling around these core human skills.

HOW TECHNOLOGY IS USED IN THE HOME

There are also views that one of the challenges of developing foundational human skills such as empathy and context sensing is the negative impact of social media and *technology saturation*. As the MIT sociologist Sherry Turkle has argued, there is mounting evidence that, even before the overload of technology during the pandemic, how people interacted with technology was affecting the development of their foundational human skills.[14] Her view is that when children and adults spend a significant amount of their time engaged with online games and social media their face-to-face foundational human skills begin to atrophy. The short volleys of interaction on social media do little to develop social skills. In part that's because the evolutionary benefits that humans have developed in empathy and collaboration have to be reinforced by subtle individual learning and feedback. Contrast, for example, a child's conversations with the Amazon Alexa virtual assistant and with a grandparent. In interacting with Alexa, the child may be tempted to bark instructions and possibly be rude to the machine. Alexa simply replies back in a steady, dignified manner. Any child who mimicked such an interaction with their grandparents would likely be reprimanded for rude behaviour.

STRESS AT WORK

There is also the challenge of the design of work. Most adults learn a great deal at work, so we could imagine that adults will learn foundational human skills in the workplace. Yet whether skills such as empathy and creativity are developed or used is highly sensitive to how a person is feeling. When you feel under pressure – when you feel you've been treated unfairly, for example – the hippocampus (the part of your brain's limbic system that is associated with emotion) is much less able to engage in empathic listening or appreciating the context of a situation. Your brain, in other words, closes down to learning or performing skills like listening and empathizing.

That's a real wake-up call for redesigning work. If in the redesign of work you create workplaces that – even unintentionally – produce high levels of stress then you are creating barriers to developing and using foundational human skills. That is why it is so important to understand the role that flexible working practices, collaborative cultures and fair processes play in facilitating the development and use of foundational human skills.

New ways to develop human skills

Whilst foundational human skills like empathy are crucial for many jobs, they are fiendishly difficult to develop. Mark Atkinson, CEO of the technology learning group Mursion, has been studying these human skills in leaders. As he told me:

> What makes a good leader in terms of human skills is a small set of things they do that builds up the best in colleagues and customers. Those that do it well, who engage in really active listening, are able to de-escalate emotional tension in a group situation, can yield for the sake of getting to yes and are able to manage the diversity in the group. They are also good at drawing out extreme introverts who can be really deep thinkers. They create space for them and recognize their talents are unique.

The challenge is that, unlike many cognitive and technical skills, foundational human skills cannot be learnt in a rules-based way, they take repetition and practice. Yet there is more clarity about the indicators of success. As Mark told me, 'Studies using sentiment analysis of voice patterns can predict those people who are more socially effective.' This sentiment analysis has analysed, for example, the communication patterns in the medical emergency room – the extent to which medical staff are condescending or rude, the patterns of nodding and tracking and the synchronicity between them – either 'dancing with each other' or 'in combat'. Those who were 'dancing' made better decisions, worked better together and had higher indicators of success.

How best to develop these skills? This is how Mark sees it:

> Building job-related social skills for a work environment requires an immersive learning experience, rehearsed in situations as close as possible to the real job, with lots of opportunities for practice. This kind of skill development is essentially a process of trial and error, where we behave in a certain way, get feedback through subtle social cues and try again. Practice creates the muscle of habit.

By harnessing learning technologies, learning experts are discovering new ways to scale the improvement of human skills. These training programmes don't rely on expensive classroom-based coaching, but rather use a combination of virtual reality and artificial intelligence with human trainers. Take a programme that gives people a chance to listen to and interact with a difficult customer or employee. It's a classic role-play training process – but in this case the difficult customer or employee is a virtual-reality avatar. The learning design team has figured out how to mimic a stressful working environment in such a plausible way that it tricks the brain into believing the VR experience is real. Trainees interact with the difficult customer and then practise across a number of different contexts, going through a process of trial and error as they converse with an AI-driven avatar. Over time they receive both objective and subjective feedback about their progress and so learn to create the fluency of conversation so crucial to foundational human skills. That's been important for the US-based hotel company Best Western International, which has used this type of training to upskill more than 35,000 employees in expressing empathy for customers and taking the steps to immediately solve customer problems.

Insight: How IBM makes developmental pathways visible

If your redesign of work is to be capable of supporting technology transitions then understanding how employees feel about this transition, predicting the pathways of automation and supporting employees to upskill and reskill will be key. There is another way that your employees will flourish and that's through the type of jobs they do. An important insight about the redesign of work is that it's on-the-job experience that can really support people to develop not only skills that the current job requires but also skills for future jobs.

But it turns out that jobs don't have equivalent skill development potential. Some are like escalators – the experience of being on them moves people up – whilst others are cul-de-sacs, the dead-end jobs that go nowhere. The challenge for executive and workers is distinguishing the cul-de-sacs from the escalators.[15]

ESCALATOR JOBS

For many professional jobs the pathways of upward mobility are highly visible. That's not always the case in medium- and low-skilled jobs. And it's these types of jobs where visible escalators can be particularly crucial. To understand this better, a study traced the trajectories of 100,000 US employees.[16] Encouragingly, the researchers found that half of those studied moved up into higher-wage jobs. Escalator jobs that created gateways to higher paid jobs included a wide range of positions including customer service, product sales, advertising sales, computer support specialists and vocational nurses.

What these escalator jobs had in common was they created opportunities to develop foundational human skills such as listening, communication, empathy, judgement and decision making. It turns out these skills, whilst important in many types of jobs, play a key role in unlocking the value of technical skills. Indeed, without them an individual cannot entirely use their technical skills. And part of the importance of these foundational human skills is that, unlike technical skills, which often have a short shelf life, they are valuable over the course of a lifetime of work.

It is possible for companies to both identify and utilize these escalators and gateway jobs. Take IBM, which has developed and now deploys a chatbot known as Myca (an acronym for My Career Advisor). This uses a range of real-time internal and external data (including data from IBM's HR system, internal opportunity boards and external labour-market data) to converse with employees about their current and future skill development. Using natural language technology, Myca describes the employee's current skill profile, shows them gateway jobs and highlights how the skills gap can be filled.

IBM – *questions for reflection*
Consider the jobs in your own company – what are the 'escalator' jobs in your business? Is this something that managers and employees are aware of – and if not, would an advantage be gained by identifying and communicating them?

Insight: How TCS enables employees to flag their skills and networks

If your employees are to flourish then the redesign of work has to create clear pathways of development and ways for employees to flag their skills and demonstrate what they've learnt to others. Typically a college degree has been a 'signalling device' for demonstrating learning – but corporations are now designing work so that an employee's learning can be signalled with ease.

At TCS there is a focus on understanding and calibrating both foundational human skills and technical skills. As Ramkumar

Chandrasekaran told me, 'Across the company the Knome internal platform supports the firm's 500,000 employees to track their skill development, to use online training to boost and broaden their skills, and then to build their reputation through skill badging.' An employee who has developed a particular skill can add a 'badge' to their profile to communicate their competence to others. From a corporate perspective, these credentials are collated and used to assess the extent and depth of skill development across the corporation.

The skills of collaborating with others and being cooperative is a significant productivity element for many TCS roles. In order to encourage and support this the company created ways to badge these important skills. Rather than track email use – which in general is discouraged as an internal collaborative tool, the connections within the firm's collaborative platform, Knome, are assessed. These connections can be microblogs (often less than a hundred words), such as, 'Hey, I've been working on this problem and found that this is the solution.' They can be longer blog posts of up to 2,000 words where employees share a more substantial description of a point of view or an explanation. For example, 'I'm working on a cloud-computing project at the moment and these are my five learnings . . .' These posts tend to be in-depth and often highly technical.

The type of connections within the platform are also important in assessing and then badging collaboration. Connections are measured by their *distance*, in terms of who people reach out to and who reach out to them. Are they in the same function, business or geography (short-distance connections) or are they in a different function, business or geography (long-distance connections)? These connections are also measured by their *vibrancy* – how often do people interact with a person's blogs or microblogs?

Networks between people with similar interests are seen as an important element of collaboration. These types of networks are named *spheres* and are the communities of interest that employees become part of. Some spheres are about personal passion – cooking, yoga and photography. Other spheres are work topics – cloud computing and data analytics are particularly popular spheres. These spheres are places of exchange and learning. An employee who wants to become certified in cloud computing, for example, can join a specialist cloud-computing sphere and ask the members questions: 'Where's a good place for me to start?' 'What certificates are the most helpful?' 'How much time do I need to put aside to learn this new area?'

The analytics underpinning these network measures of distance and vibrancy are made available to individuals and to groups. By taking a closer look at how these networks are operating in real time, individuals gain important feedback about who they are giving advice to and from whom they are receiving it. Using this data, they can determine whether they are building or depleting their own networks – for example, to what extent are their networks becoming homogeneous in the sense that they are habitually reaching out to the same people? And to what extent are they becoming less or more diverse?

Teams can also take a look at the aggregate data from their members to get a sense of networks and where knowledge is flowing. From this they can build the sort of network schema we looked at in Figure 4. These aggregate data have been used, for example, to shape corporate policy on how best to encourage cross-functional and cross-business connections.

TCS – questions for reflection
TCS's experience raises three questions for reflection. What are the means by which you are enabling employees to communicate skill development? Are there means by which, like TCS, you have created learning communities that they can easily engage with? What is your view of the way TCS measures and communicates the extent of connections – is this something that you can learn from for your company?

*Insight: How Microsoft develops skills by reaching out
into the community*

A final way of testing whether your redesign model will support technology transitions is to consider not only the extent to which it is capable of developing these crucial technological skills *inside* the company, but also whether it is able to do so *outside* the company.

Something to consider in your model for redesigning work is the breadth of the potential talent markets the design of work is capable of tapping into. The mistake would be to take an insular approach – focusing solely on your own company and current employees. As we saw when considering the demographic trends, many industrialized countries will inevitably enter a tight labour market for talent and high-value skills, so the pipeline of *future* employees could be as important as the current employees.

In my view companies can play a positive role in the world by broadening their talent-development initiatives.[17] There is an opportunity to more tightly align the redesign of work to the agenda for corporate social responsibility. Here is how: across the world billions of people are in need of higher-paying, higher-mobility, better jobs. And in order to confront this desperate need on a global scale, every company can and should play a role in looking beyond their own boundaries and current employees to their wider community. This is a theme that has been top of the agenda as I co-chair the World Economic Forum's Future Council on the New Agenda for Work, Wages and Job Creation.[18] In early 2021 the council report was published and in it we argued that businesses had a crucial and far-reaching role to play in building global skill sets beyond their own current employees.

BUILDING DIGITAL SKILLS IN LOCAL COMMUNITIES

Reaching out into the community to develop skills was the decision the leadership team at Microsoft took. In 2020 they were faced with a significant business imperative – they needed rapid expansion of the company's cloud services provision. Making this a reality meant building data centres in places ranging from populous national capitals like Dublin to mid-size cities such as Des Moines, Iowa (population just over 200,000) to remote settlements like Boydton, Virginia (population about 400). The crucial job skills for these new locations would be data-centre management, with particular responsibilities in systems administration and troubleshooting.

In any labour market these are tough skills to recruit for. And they're unlikely to exist in the local populations in some of these remote areas. Some are also places to which few current Microsoft employees would be willing to relocate, and among those who do, the retention rates anyway tend to be poor. The Microsoft team embraced this challenge by expanding its view of who could do these jobs, and by helping create new pools of local talent. They began with four locations and by 2021 had expanded this to eleven – including in other countries such as Ireland.

As Portia Wu, Microsoft's managing director of US public policy, told me, the key to this initiative has been bringing together the various stakeholders. For instance, in Boydton and in Des Moines the company worked with local community colleges to create new Microsoft data centre academies (DCAs). These colleges then trained students to work both in Microsoft facilities and other businesses with similar digital needs. Each DCA has run programmes with cohorts of between fifteen and twenty students, and by 2021 over 200 students had graduated. Some have gone on to join Microsoft, whilst others took their skills to related companies, helping to expand the overall technology environment in these regions.

LAUNCHING A GLOBAL SKILLS INITIATIVE

Taking a wider perspective on developing skills was the driving force that allowed the executive team at Microsoft to launch a global skills initiative in early 2020. They began by creating a 'digital skills equity map' that showed the location of digital skills across the world. From this they discovered that locations with low digital skills levels also inevitably had poor broadband internet connections and limited foundational digital competence.

In the light of the digital skills equity map, the executive team set a goal to bring digital skills to 25 million people across the world. This was supported by using Microsoft's own internal resources whilst also building new partnerships. Internally, the job-posting data from LinkedIn was combined with the skills profiles of millions of developers on GitHub to build live data streams. Using this aggregate data, the team created a granular description of in-demand jobs which enabled them to build a navigation system. These systems gave job seekers a deeper understanding of the jobs that would be valuable in the future and proved to be a real driver of the motivation to upskill.

In order to support those on the escalator to a better job, the team at Microsoft also worked with a range of partners to provide free access to learning modules, enable low-cost skill certifications and provide free job-seeking tools. In addition, Microsoft made available $20 million in cash grants to support non-profit organizations which support people to upskill.

Microsoft – questions for reflection
As you look forward, what are the skills that are going to be most tough for your business to recruit for in the short, medium and long term? Consider the Microsoft community initiatives – do you have any current community-based initiatives that would be capable of supporting skill development of future employees? And would this be a good time, as you go about redesigning work, to more closely align your work models with your corporate social responsibility agenda?

<u>Action #11</u>
Model and test that the model supports technology transitions

- Take another look at the schema in Figure 13. Do you know for your key jobs' families what the likely pathways of automation are – and do employees have this insight?
- To what extent does the redesign of work factor in the development of foundational human skills? Are there opportunities for you to creatively deploy technology for this?
- Do you know where the escalator jobs are, and are you ensuring that these are used to create mobility?
- Does the model of work create within it opportunities for people to communicate their skills and learning?
- Could the redesign of work be more creative about tapping into the skills of the wider community? Are there ways you can leverage capabilities in your communities to widen the future pool of talent?

Model and Test: That the model of work is fair and just

Is the model for the redesign of work fair and just, is it likely to build, maintain or deplete trust among employees?

Of course, when redesigning work, no executive deliberately sets out to deplete trust and create unfair practices but it could become an unintended consequence.

Businesses are facing a time of significant disruption, ambiguities and unforeseen events. In navigating through this period, employee trust will be a crucial asset. High-trust organizations are more agile and flexible, and employees of high-trust organizations are significantly less stressed, more energetic and productive, more engaged and satisfied, and less likely to experience burnout.[19] Importantly, people in high-trust organizations are more likely to benefit from 'psychological safety' – they feel able to talk about their real feelings, to challenge others and to have confidence that their group will not embarrass, ridicule or reject their ideas and views. They feel more able to 'speak up'.

Creating a model of work that is fair and just will be crucial.

Make sure everyone *benefits from the redesign*

Looking back to the early phases of the pandemic, when many companies were in the 'unfreeze' state, there was much conversation about listening to employees and their specific needs and also excitement about the possibilities of changing working practices. Perhaps, executives debated, people could work from home more, or have work designed in a way that created more opportunities to be engaged in tasks that required focus and undisturbed time.

Yet, as the consequences became clearer, another narrative began to emerge. There was growing unease that the very aspects of redesign that seemed to work so well for some would not work for others; there would be losers as well as winners. We began to see the first signals of unintended consequences.

PRIMARY CARERS

Executives fretted that in this shift to working from home, it was carers who seemed to get the worst deal. And, as described earlier, in some households it was women who were putting in more domestic time, and were more likely to take homeworking rather than office options. If carers (either men or women) stayed at home when others returned to the office, the concern was that this would impact on their longer-term promotion prospects.

YOUNGER WORKERS

There was also a growing realization that for some groups of employees – particularly younger workers, who often shared their home space with flatmates, the chance to work at home was not a big draw and could be seen as a disadvantage. Also, removing the chance to learn through observation put them in danger of losing that important connection to more experienced people and their knowledge.

THOSE FOR WHOM HOMEWORKING IS NOT AN OPTION

Beyond the excitement about homeworking, the simple truth was that for many workers this was not, and never would be, an option. That is true for doctors and nurses in hospitals and care workers in the community; for people working in the manufacturing, delivery and supply chain; and for the millions of people engaged as platform workers in companies like Deliveroo or Uber. In fact, as the 2021 census survey in the UK (which took place during the pandemic on 21 March) reported, only 46 per cent of employed people said they were working from home that day (in the US the figure was about 47 per cent). That still left a lot of people who weren't working from home. Imagine if you worked on the assembly line of a car plant and on two days a week you saw the offices of your administrative colleagues empty because they were working from home – how would you feel?

In the early phases of the pandemic I saw how many companies, when they began experimenting with new approaches to work, typically allowed managers to drive the process on an ad hoc basis. Some executives left it to individual managers to talk with their teams to make it work. On the face of it, this makes sense, but over time, with no guiding principles or collaborative decision making, inevitably this gave rise to accusations of unfairness. As it played out, different departments and teams were afforded different degrees of flexibility and freedom. Some began to feel unfairly treated.

The tough decisions to be faced

Whilst the redesign of work has great opportunities, it also has the potential to create significant possibilities for unfairness. To understand these possibilities more, I asked executives in a series of workshops, webinars and interviews which judgement calls they thought could, if not handled properly, result in feelings of unfairness. Here are some example responses: 'How do we manage home/office flexibility?' 'Who should be in the office and who should work from home?' 'How do we build a system of time flexibility that acknowledges the caring responsibilities of parents of young children but does not put an undue burden on those without caring responsibilities?' 'How do we know that people working at home are productive rather than shirking, and how do we ensure that we don't put in place monitoring systems that assume they are not trusted?' 'How do we balance office work, where flexibility of working from home is a possibility, with other jobs where there is no flexibility around place?'

The factors that influence fairness and justice

Think of an employee faced with a situation where fairness will be in issue. Take two examples: Amy, a single person without caring responsibilities in a group where two of her co-workers have young children to care for, and Eric, an assembly-line worker with office-based colleagues.

How do Amy and Eric decide whether they have been treated fairly? It could be, for example, that Amy feels it's unfair she has to cover for her colleagues with caring responsibilities, and Eric feels it's unfair he doesn't have the flexibility that his office-based colleagues have. Over many years various studies have teased out what influences perceptions of fairness. It turns out this has not just one factor but several. And as you consider whether the model for the redesign of work you have in mind is fair, you will need to reference each of these factors – outcomes, procedures and interactions.

WAS THE *OUTCOME* FAIR?

When Amy and Eric think about their working experiences they will consider whether the outcome (what researchers call distributed fairness) is in their judgement equitable. Perhaps Amy feels that she is being treated unfairly because on three occasions in the last week she was asked to put in extra hours because the two people with caring responsibilities had to leave early to look after their children. Whilst Amy is happy to do this occasionally, she is beginning to feel unfairly treated and taken for granted. She is beginning to wonder whether this will become a norm, whether it will be she who has to step up whenever there is a crunch in projects. Eric might feel he is being treated unfairly for very different reasons. He could notice, as mentioned, that the offices are empty on some days, so he cannot simply pop into the office with a quick question should an issue arise. In addition, Eric and his colleagues might feel that, compared to the office workers, they are getting the raw end of the deal.

WAS THE *PROCEDURE* FAIR?

Clearly, it's the outcome that is the most obvious factor when we think about fairness. But behind these feelings of fairness about the outcome is a sense of the process that was used to reach that outcome. We judge a process to be fair on a range of criteria: Is it consistent over time and between people? Do we trust that it is not biased by the self-interest of the decision makers? Is it accurate in the sense of being based on reliable information? Does it represent the needs, values and outlook of all those it will affect? Is it ethical in the sense that it is compatible with our own moral and ethical values?

What is important about the impact of procedural fairness is that, whilst it is about a single process, when we feel we have been treated unfairly with regard to this single process our reactions are directed to the whole organization and every process.

Let's take a closer look at Amy's situation to examine this. Imagine that Amy was not consulted about covering when colleagues are looking after their children. It was simply assumed that she would do so. She will see that the procedure, or rather lack of one, is unfair. What might be a fairer process? It could be that the whole team sits down to discuss the issue beforehand. As a team they can decide on a number of possible ways forward; perhaps those with caring responsibilities give as much notice of unavailability as possible, or arrange among themselves to job-share, or work longer days and/ or a shorter week. And if people like Amy are asked to step in, then they are able to take time off to compensate.

We can play out the procedural options for Eric as well. Like Amy, he is more likely to feel he has been unfairly treated if there is no procedure in place. The simplest of procedures would be to acknowledge to Eric and the others on the assembly line that office workers have flexibility about the place of work and assembly workers do not. But are there opportunities to create flexibility for assembly-line workers like Eric – not around place, of course, but around time? It might be possible, for example, to use the redesign of work as an opportunity to look at time flexibility: working longer shifts in the day so that the week is four days rather than five; or moving to a four-day week; or working seven days on and three days off.

WAS THE *INTERACTION* JUST AND FAIR?

The third factor that influences our feelings of fairness and justice is the manner of the interactions with team leaders and managers. This is the human side of organizational practices – the way the manager behaves towards the recipients. Do employees feel they are being treated with politeness, honesty and respect?[20]

You can get a sense of the importance of this in a study that Jerald Greenberg, professor of management and human resources at Ohio State University, conducted.[21] He looked at how pay cuts were handled at two manufacturing plants (A and B). The vice-presidents took slightly different approaches. In plant A the vice-president called a meeting at the end of the working week and announced that the company would implement a 15 per cent pay cut, across the board, for ten weeks. He very briefly explained why, thanked employees and answered a few questions – the whole episode was over in fifteen minutes. In plant B, where an identical pay cut was being communicated, the company vice-president handled things slightly differently. He first told the affected employees that other cost-saving options such as layoffs had been considered, but that a pay cut seemed to be the least unpalatable choice. He then took an hour and a half to address employees' questions and concerns, and he repeatedly expressed regret about having to take this step. Even the scale of these interactional differences made an impact. Greenberg found that during the following ten-week period, employee theft was nearly 80 per cent lower in Plant B than at Plant A, and employees were fifteen times less likely to resign.

So, we can assume that if Amy is simply informed by email or by a harassed and overworked manager that she is expected to cover for her colleagues with caring responsibilities, she is much more likely to feel that she has been treated unfairly than if her manager sits down with her, shows empathy with her situation, listens to her point of view and then describes why they have concluded that she has to cover. The same is true for Eric. He is more likely to feel that he has been treated fairly if his supervisor meets him and his workmates to talk through the issues, is empathetic to their situation and acknowledges that their deal is not the same as the office workers', before telling them the decision that the executive team have come to.

Why it's so hard to be fair

On the face of it, these three factors of fairness seem relatively straightforward – ensure the outcome and procedure are fair and that interactions involved are empathic. But the reality is that these qualities are often hard to deliver – and ever more so during the pandemic. In part that's because many tough decisions were made at a time when the resources to make these decisions fair were stretched. This was one of the issues the executives in my Future of Work Consortium addressed in the series of workshops in October 2020. There was clear evidence that these were tough times and for each of the three factors there were significant strains.

OUTCOME FAIRNESS – THE PRESSURE TO GET
THINGS DONE

As managers grappled with the impact of the pandemic and its after-math, many felt under real pressure to get the job done and make quick decisions. As a consequence there were times when they cut corners and failed to represent the needs of everyone. They were operating under conditions of significant uncertainty and ambiguity, and faced with an unpredictable future, it was hard to know exactly what to do for the best. At the same time, employees were feeling anxious and unprepared: Would they lose their job? Would a program or machine take over a significant slice of their work? A survey conducted in the midst of the pandemic reported that 83 per cent of employees said they feared becoming unemployed – citing the likely causes as the gig economy, a looming recession, a lack of skills, cheaper foreign competitors, immigrants who will work for less, automation, or jobs being moved to other countries.[22] As companies move into the next phase of redesigning work, it is clear that skilled managers will play a central role in ensuring outcomes are fair and, as we will explore in Chapter 5, there is much that can be done to assist managers – both by restructuring their jobs and by providing much needed support and development opportunities.

PROCEDURAL FAIRNESS – THE PLIGHT OF OTHERS

During the pandemic, many workers were either temporarily or permanently laid off. This inevitably had an impact on those who remained, sometimes called 'survival guilt'. Layoffs can also create in those employees who remain a sense that they've lost control, the fate of their ex-peers sending a clear signal that hard work and good performance do not guarantee immunity. Indeed, one 2002 study found that, after a layoff, survivors experienced a 41 per cent decline in job satisfaction, a 36 per cent decline in organizational commitment and a 20 per cent decline in job performance.[23]

So, even when the process was fair, there were times when people were too anxious to acknowledge this. That puts a real emphasis on engaging employees across your company in conversations about what is happening and how they are feeling. And, as we will see in Chapter 5, the 'leader's narrative' can do much to lay out a future that people can feel positive about and engage with.

INTERACTIONAL FAIRNESS – THE CHALLENGE OF REMOTE WORK

There can be significant barriers to managers' empathy and the integrity of their message. That is especially true for managers and colleagues who work remotely. As people work remotely so their support networks reduce, and so too did the opportunities for those encounters when managers could seek in-the-moment guidance from colleagues, or speak informally to a team member over a coffee. During the pandemic for many the conversion from face-to-face to virtual communication hampered these sensitive conversations. That's because much of the way we naturally empathize with one another is through visual signals – we can gauge someone's emotional state with a quick glance. Such interpretation becomes much harder via a computer monitor or phone screen. During the pandemic this combination of time stress, uncertainty and isolation resulted in people finding it more difficult to create a fair process.

As post-pandemic ways of working are designed, often with an emphasis on both face-to-face and virtual work, these issues of interactional fairness will have to be addressed. That means bringing employees together in ways that make them feel connected, even in a virtual environment, and being more intentional about each of the factors of fairness. Engaging people in conversations about the choices and trade-offs they face and acknowledging that in these times of uncertainty, the executive team won't always get it right.

Some executive teams are working hard to achieve this. They are giving employees time to reflect and think about their situation, and making sure there is time to have their voice heard. They are listening and sharing stories that frame the dilemmas people face so they can understand them more deeply. They have framed the redesign of work as a series of experiments from which everyone is learning, not as a one-off intervention, but rather as part of a long-term collaboration.

Insight: How Brit Insurance creates a fair process

This transparency and involvement is a core belief of the CEO of Brit Insurance, Matthew Wilson, and chief engagement officer Lorraine Denny. The company is based in the heart of the City of London with employees in the US and Bermuda.

GOING BEYOND THE 'USUAL SUSPECTS'

The team at Brit Insurance had begun in the autumn of 2020 to design a process that would refresh their core values. To make the design and implementation of these new ways of working as inclusive as possible, they made a bold choice. Rather than involving the 'usual suspects' in the process, they chose 10 per cent of the whole employee group at random, from receptionists to senior underwriters and from all three office locations to become part of a design community.

By the spring of 2021 it was clear that most of the company's activities would have to swing from face to face to virtual, and this presented an opportunity not only to refresh the core values, but also to focus on the redesign of work. During the following six months, the design community was divided into peer learning teams of six employees – each drawn from multiple divisions, levels, and generational cohorts – who worked together virtually across the company.

BUILDING DEEP KNOWLEDGE ABOUT THE FUTURE

The process began by building a deeper and shared understanding of how work was changing and how it might change over the coming decade. The community looked, for example, at the impact of technology on Brit Insurance jobs, how recent developments in technological connectivity could create productivity opportunities and how longevity and population growth would shape their insurance products. They took a closer look at societal trends and how family structures would put pressure on some of the traditional ways of working. They also used diagnostic tools to profile and then share with their peer learning team their own working capabilities and preferences.

Armed with this deep knowledge of the future of work and their own capabilities, the team members examined how other companies were responding. They discussed the trends they observed, the practices they had seen other companies adopt and what this would mean for how Brit could best prepare for the future.

PITCHING IDEAS

All the teams from across the whole design community then came together in a half-day virtual 'hackathon', during which they discussed their ideas and began to prepare a presentation of the one or two ideas they found most exciting. They then pitched their ideas to Matthew and Lorraine. This gave the executive team a chance to look across the whole business, to get a better view of what people really wanted, and to judge the enthusiasm and energy behind these ideas.

The teams proposed to significantly increase the learning opportunities within Brit Insurance, to continue with the idea of community learning and to do more to support those cross-functional moves that would create stronger links across the parts of the business. They also wanted to widen the idea of peer learning to include spending time in other companies both within and outside the insurance sector. Over the course of the following year, the teams explored with the executive committee how to turn these proposals into action and to support this the chief financial officer,

Gavin Wilkinson, became a crucial backer. For example, with regard to resources, the team realized they would need a person working with them to manage the rotations into other companies. Wilkinson was enthusiastic about the idea and became their board sponsor in the implementation phase.

As Lorraine commented:

The project absolutely had legs, there was a real sense of excitement. One of the great benefits was that a broad spectrum of people got involved – so many important relationships were made. Everyone was equal to each other – and everyone was involved with learning. This was a huge benefit – people enjoyed building these relationships and engaging on a level playing field. There were also benefits to being virtual – the project demonstrated how relationships could end up being stronger. People could 'see' into each other's lives – they got a sense of their homes, their children, their pets. The bonds got stronger. They felt part of each other's world. They'd start by saying, 'How are you – how are you doing?' People learnt more about each other in their totality – not just as workers.

CREATING THE 'BRIT PLAYBOOK'

To widen the understanding of how work would change, the community developed the 'Brit Playbook'. This described some of the new ways employees would now work together. The whole experience, Lorraine told me at the time, 'demonstrated that actually everybody has something to say, and everybody enjoys and wants to be part of this experience'.

Over the course of the following year the design community formed strong networks with each other, which traversed the whole company. They also significantly increased the knowledge and expertise in redesigning work. That meant that when the executive team debated issues such as how to create flexibility around place and time, there was already in place a group of 'champions' who could spread the message and engage their colleagues across the company. I asked Dr Anna Gurun, who led the project for HSM Advisory, what we had learnt. She pointed to three lessons:

> First, the process of co-creation ensured that people felt account-able and had a sense of ownership over the change that happened. Being part of a learning group with peers meant that people were more committed to their learning as they didn't want to let others down. Second, because the ideas came directly from employees, they used what they had learnt from the programme and their experience at Brit to generate truly bold ideas, building off each other. Third, the project really demonstrated the power of leader-ship in taking a stand and promising to implement one key action from employees – without knowing what that would be. It really demonstrated courage and a capacity to be innovative.

Brit Insurance – questions for reflection

What's your view of going 'beyond the usual suspects' and, as you go about redesigning work, bringing in people from all levels and parts of the company for project work? As you think about redesigning work for the future, would there be any advantage in taking the route that Brit Insurance took to upskill people across the business in understanding future trends? Consider how the CEO and CFO of Brit became actively involved in this process. What were the benefits of this and is this an approach that could work in your company?

Insight: Virtual trust at Artemis Connection

Artemis Connection is an almost completely virtual strategy con-sultancy. Christy Johnson, the company's founder and CEO, has thought a great deal about how to deliver fairness in a virtual environment. I asked her if she had any lessons for companies embarking on the journey of redesigning work. She made three proposals.

First, start with your core principles. As Christy says: 'Establish trust and ethics as core principles of the team. And be sure that trust is given, not earned.'

Second, be intentional about the design of the communication processes: make clear when people connect, how they connect and why they connect. As Christy remarks: 'When you are working in virtual teams it's so much easier for people to "hide" or not be visible. So you need to schedule communications, on video where possible. Also, try to reproduce those serendipitous conversations – pick up the phone and ask, "Hey how are you?" As she went on to explain, 'We have lost the "management by walking" approach, so we need to support managers in a virtual environment.' Like others I've spoken with, Christy favours 'behavioural nudges' to support managers to do the right thing. So, for example, they produce a standard list of questions for team leaders to ask their team members about their motivations and interests.

Third, build fairness and trust in the everyday team processes. Here is what works for them: 'Schedule team problem-solving sessions, and at project close-out meetings ask questions like "Did we act with integrity?" "Did we build trust?"'

Action #12
Model and Test that the model of work is fair and just

- Take a look at the key roles. In terms of employee experiences are there areas where there is potential for issues of justice and fairness to arise?
- Consider the model of redesigned work. How will this change the employee experience?
- Look closely at all three factors. The outcome: in the judgement of employees will the outcome be seen to be fair? The procedure: have you designed a process that will be consistent over time, is not biased and is accurate?

The manner of the interaction: will your plans for action enable managers and team leaders to communicate this in a fair way?

- What are your guiding principles with regard to justice and fairness? Have you designed the process in a way that co-creates with others?

5. Act and Create

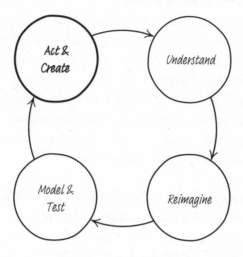

The redesign of work is fundamentally about action and creation. Everything we have learnt so far has been leading up to this moment. There is no point understanding your company, reimagining it and modelling and testing the new design if you don't have the commitment to, or can't get your employees and managers to buy into the process and create the change. To create a new way of working that is future-proofed, that engages and excites employees and that enables the organization to grow and prosper requires positive action. As I look at those companies that have been successful at doing this, I can see that they embrace a multistakeholder approach and engage managers, employees and leaders.

The organizations that have successfully implemented this stage have all paid close attention to the pivotal role of good managers. Core managerial skills include both scheduling and managing when and where people work, and managing team members' performance and careers. As I have learnt from the executive team at the Australian telecoms company Telstra, one way of supporting managers is to fundamentally redesign their role to give more time for these rather different activities. And as Standard Chartered bank has shown, supporting managers can also mean making significant investments in their development.

Next, rather than seeing the redesign of work as a hierarchical, top-down process, these companies have often embraced co-creation. Like the executives at Brit Insurance, they have encouraged employees to engage in the debate and used these insights and energy to build momentum across the networks of the firm. Engaging employees is a foundational tool of my advisory practice HSM Advisory, and for the Swedish technology company Ericsson this opened up an important opportunity to create energy for redesigning work.

Balanced with this need for co-creation is an acknowledgement that, as employees consider what could be an uncertain future, it is the leader's narrative that can create meaning and focus. As we complete these four steps of the redesign of work we will look at how one software company – Sage – went through the whole process and what they learnt along the way.

Act and Create: The pivotal role of good managers
- Insight: Telstra
- Insight: Standard Chartered
- Action #13

Act and Create: The power of co-creation
- Insight: Ericsson
- Action #14

Act and Create: The leader's narrative
- Action #15

Act and Create: The four steps of redesigning work
- Insight: Sage
- Action #16

Act and Create: The pivotal role of good managers

Good managers are the thread that connects people and work. As you look back to the many examples I have shared of what companies are doing, the role of managers, though not necessarily always made apparent, is nevertheless crucial. It's they who manage workflows, think through the team schedules of place and block out time for focused work. It is they who consider whether these schedules meet team members' needs, whether the tasks their colleagues are performing are pushing them into new skills or simply repeating already developed skills. It is they who are making calls about issues of fairness across the wider group and treating people with respect and dignity. And it is they who are coaching others to upskill in their current role, or counselling them to reskill to move to their next potential role.

It is clear that good managers are crucial to redesigning work. But that's rather odd because for many years the focus has been on leaders, to the extent that some have asked what managers are for. And when managers are often referred to as the 'permafrost', then it's obvious this is a group not seen to be at the forefront of redesigning work. So, here is the challenge: whilst managers will become ever more important, the design and support of their own work has failed to keep up with this growing significance. And until it does, they will not be in a position to support these important and fundamental changes that come with redesigning work. Let's take a closer look at how to best acknowledge and support the pivotal role of managers.

The work of the manager – a story of fragmentation and overload

Diane Gherson was IBM's chief resources officer from 2013 to 2020, serving CEO Ginni Rometty. She and I jointly explored the issue of managers and their role in late March 2021 in an HSM Advisory webinar, where we asked executives from sixty companies from around the world two questions: 'How would you describe the everyday experience of being a manager?' and 'What do you see as changing in the manager's role post-Covid?'

The response to the first question – the current managerial role – was overwhelmingly negative. Two words stood out: 'exhausted' and 'frustrated'. One year into the pandemic, managers were beginning to fray. Of course, this fraying is not new: a 1940 study of managers reported barely twenty-three minutes without interruption, in 1965 a Swedish research team observed the role was highly fragmented, and Henry Mintzberg's famous study of the everyday experiences of managers in 1973 described unrelenting pace, many interruptions and an action focus.[1]

The fragmentation and overload of the manager's role is partly the result of a whole series of process and technical innovations beginning with process re-engineering. Then the role became more digital and the span of control widened as AI and automation augmented the manager's role by performing the repetitive administrative tasks. As internal digital platforms (like the Knome platform at TCS) developed, leaders could now interact directly with employees, leaving the manager potentially out of the loop. This was followed in some companies by the introduction of agile working, which broke down the concept of intact teams into fluid projects. This further eroded the managers' day-to-day interactions with their team members.

The result of these process and technical changes is that managers often had increased responsibilities, more pressure and less support. As you consider how to action the redesign of work, it's a good time to also think about reinventing the role of the manager.

What good managers do

Despite the challenges that managers faced, particularly during the pandemic, many did a sterling job. When we asked the webinar respondents the second question – 'What do you see as changing in the manager's role post-Covid?' – more than 80 per cent of the comments were positive, with three words at the centre: 'coaching', 'well-being' and 'communication'.

During the pandemic good managers coached and communicated. That was clear from a Microsoft study that analysed the data from daily employee pulse surveys. These revealed a consistent pattern: when managers stepped up to help teams prioritize, nurture team culture and support work–life balance, their teams felt more connected to one another, and more positive about their work.[2]

The team at TCS found the same. They reviewed the daily analytic data collected on managers' interactions and team performance. An aspect of analysis was the managers' communication style: Did they send daily or weekly emails? Did they prefer project boards or face-to-face meetings? Did they meet individual team members or have full team meetings? They then related this communication style to team performance. And, as Ashok Krish, who heads the digital workplace unit at TCS, told me, 'We have discovered that those managers who initiated frequent one-to-one discussions with their team members had the highest-performing teams.'

As Diane and I concluded, these good managers have made four important mindset shifts.

First, they've moved away from the traditional hierarchical and manager-led idea of 'My team is here to make *me* successful' to a more team-based mindset: 'I'm here to make *my team* successful'. Good managers do this in a variety of ways – by supporting people to be engaged, motivated and skilled, by coaching and giving feedback, and by creating a supportive and inclusive work environment.

Second, they've made a mindset shift from hoarding resources to sharing resources. That means, for example, a shift from considering their role as 'I'm focused on my team members' next promotion and *controlling* their movement out of the unit' to a more open, sharing and collaborative mindset: 'I'm coaching my team to *grow* and spot opportunities for them to move inside and outside the unit'. This mindset shift of putting the needs of the team first was in place before the pandemic. The impact of the pandemic was to reconfigure where and when people work, and that pivot created more complex scheduling needs and required a more intentional design of workflows.

Third, as more companies made the move from *structured* teams to *fluid* teams, good managers shifted from 'I manage and control an intact team' to 'My teams are fluid, with members working on projects in other units, and with people borrowed from other units'.

Fourth, as there is more flexibility around time and place, good managers shifted their mindset from 'I organize jobs by resourcing work from within the team to be done within the office' to the management of people in rather different circumstances – 'Work can be done from anywhere, the focus is on tasks and projects, and I can leverage talent from within and outside the company'. That shift has significant implications for how team performance is managed and assessed. From 'I assess performance through *direct oversight* of work and annual goal setting and assessment' to 'I focus on *outcomes* through ongoing prioritization of work and coaching'.

Here are some ideas about how companies have supported managers to make these four mindset shifts.

Insight: How Telstra reinvented the role of managers

Changing the manager's role was seen to be a crucial part of a wider organizational change at Telstra. The initiative was led by Alex Badenoch, the chief human resource officer, who worked with CEO Andy Penn on the goal to transform the US$16.3 billion Australian telecoms giant (employing more than 32,000 people) to become more customer-focused and fast paced.

The executive team at Telstra had taken the same path that Diana Gherson and Ginni Rometty (then CHRO and CEO) had taken at IBM – they'd invested in process reengineering, digitalization and agile working practices. But Alex realized that to really help managers step up would take a fundamental change in the architecture of the role.

The real innovative moment came when the executive team decided to dramatically reduce the number of organization layers to three, and at the same time to split the manager job into two equal but distinct roles: *Leaders of Work* and *Leaders of People*. This model covers almost all the company's activities, from accounting to sales – but excludes field operations and call centres.

The Leaders of Work define the work, performance goals and resource plan to achieve Telstra's business outcomes, and then manage the work in agile projects. They rely on the Leaders of People to supply the talent they need.

That leaves the Leaders of People to focus exclusively on coaching and developing those in their 'chapter', typically around 200 people. Each chapter is made up of people with similar primary skills – in a sense they are communities of practice and can be located across the world. As Alex described to us, 'The role of the Leader of People is to know people beyond their work, to understand their career aspirations, to feed their minds, and create thought provocations.' It is they who support people to develop new skills which both align with the current and future skills needs whilst also showing the complementary skills that would connect and provide skill pathways to other chapters.

The accountability and performance of the Leaders of People are measured in a number of ways. A crucial measure is engagement. This includes the engagement scores from their chapter members, the Net Promoter Scores of their members and retention. Next, Leaders of People are accountable and measured on the extent of the dynamic building of capability – for example, how effectively they fulfil project requirements, the proportion of their people who were underemployed and, finally, by budget and operating costs.

Alex had three learning points for other companies embarking on this road. First, getting to this level of granularity of accountability and success measures required building a technical infrastructure. This had to be capable of creating the basic metrics the Leaders of People and the Leaders of Work needed to do their jobs. This included measurements of resource allocation, skills profiles, work demands and plans of work.

Second, her view is that in order to create space for managers to coach and support, it is important to focus on the structure of the job. Her decision was to craft these twin management roles. Other companies might take alternative approaches – but this is a challenge that has to be addressed one way or another.

Third, she believed one should not underestimate the impact that structural changes like this can have on productivity. Her view is that redesigning the role of the manager accelerated the productivity promise of digitization, AI and agile working. And crucially, it enabled Telstra to tap into the technology investments the corporation had made by removing the sclerosis of traditional bounded teams and enabling a more adaptive organization design.

Telstra – questions for reflection

As you consider the choices that Telstra made, what is your view of splitting the management role into Leaders of People and Leaders of Work? Is this something that you have done, or would consider? One of the big learning points for Alex was the importance of measurement and analytics. How are you currently measuring the impact of managers on their team – are there opportunities to widen this perspective? Are the promised productivity gains from your investment in technology being held back by – to use Alex's phrase – 'the sclerosis of traditional bounded teams'?

Insight: How IBM put more resources at managers' disposal

If managers are to fulfil their pivotal role in the redesign of work they need more resources at their disposal.

AI can offload many transactional tasks – spotting irregularities in travel and expense reports, matching candidates to job requirements and actually executing transfers without human intervention.

Together these free up managers' time to do what really makes a difference – listening, coaching, supporting skill development and so on.

Yet in terms of time, one of the real challenges for many managers is the conversations that accompany team members' salary review. When done badly, the review can create a host of fairness issues which can ultimately reduce trust. As Diana describes, during her tenure as CHRO of IBM there was much development of AI to support managers, and to use AI to offload much of the hard work managers typically do to fairly allocate salary and bonus payments. The AI algorithms use real-time data from multiple sources to calculate the pay gap between market rates and individual performance. This includes data on the market value of the employees' skills, the skill demand quantified by scraping postings from competitor job sites, the projected internal demand for the skill and the voluntary attrition rate of similar skills across the organization. Then to support managers' questions as they make their decisions, a bot is able to provide information in real time, for example about when the employee last received a pay increase or promotion, or the training courses they've taken. Together these data create a vital communication script that managers can use to share with employees the rationale for their salary and bonus payments whilst encouraging them to acquire more market-relevant skills.

The team at IBM are also supporting managers with an array of behavioural insights and nudges. For example, piecing together signals that an employee may be vulnerable to quitting; spotting patterns of non-collaborative behaviour in a team member; creating calendar reminders to celebrate a significant win or contribution.

By changing the architecture of the role and investing in AI to automate some tasks the teams at Telstra and IBM created space for managers to support employees. And as TCS's Ashok Krish reminds us, the real magic takes place in one-to-one conversations. When managers listen, empathize and coach they create those vital connections.

Insight: How Standard Chartered invests in boosting managers' skills

But what happens if managers don't have the skills and capabilities to carry out these roles that will be so crucial in the redesign of work? It is likely that your business, like many others, has invested in development for your leaders – but what of managers?

Standard Chartered is a retail bank with over 1,200 branches across seventy countries. More than 90 per cent of the bank's profit comes from Asia, Africa and the Middle East. For the executive team there was an understanding that upskilling managers would be crucial.

As Tanuj Kapilashrami, who heads human resources, explained to me:

> We'd worked a great deal on our values and what this meant for leadership behaviour. And over a period of two years we'd focused our attention on the top 1,000 leaders. We spent millions on the development of leaders but realized we needed to support people in managerial roles. It's too easy to talk about managers as the perma-frost in the business and to blame the lack of change on managers. We asked ourselves – are they really the permafrost or our biggest opportunity? We realized we'd never really invested in managers and never taken a data lens to their roles. We wanted to democratize the access to various leadership tools.

It took some creative thinking to decide how best to support the 14,000 people who manage others. The team began by changing the naming – to People Leaders. As Tanuj explained:

It's a symbolic change – but it's more than that because we began to bring them together as a community. We made the role clearer and demonstrated its importance by creating a process of accreditation. It's now a community – for example this morning we had a call between our CEO Bill Winters and the People Leaders. The quality of the challenges is high, it's a real learning opportunity. We see them as coach, convenor of capability, culture carrier.

They then went about experimenting and building prototypes.

BEHAVIOURAL NUDGES

In one experiment the executive team developed a self-diagnostic to build data on various managerial activities and then created behavioural nudges around the outcomes. Tanuj shared an example:

Looking at the hiring data for the previous week we realized that in one group, out of ten opportunities to hire, the managers had not found a single diverse person. We wanted to play back this data to the whole community so we sent out a note – 'How can we support you in making your teams more diverse?' We began to work through a series of behavioural nudges often about crucial 'moments that matter'. For example, on diverse hiring we showed the managers the points at which they were making key decisions and how they might go about thinking about these. These nudges are important, they are opportunities to shift: not to make this a moment of failing, but rather to see this as a learning opportunity.

A FOCUS ON COACHING

They also experimented with broadening the scope of coaching. The bank has a tradition going back many decades of providing coaching to their leadership cadre and training leaders to be coaches. It's one of the unique 'signatures' of the organization.

The challenge is that what works for hundreds begins to look impossible for many thousands. So the team began to experiment with the concept of supporting their own People Leaders to become coaches for others. As Tanuj explains:

> If a People Leader wants to be trained as a coach we will offer them formal accreditation and support them by paying half of the fee. The deal is we expect them to coach five other people. As people thought about their future many realized that giving feedback and coaching would be crucial and they wanted to be upskilled in this valuable capability.

What started as an original group of 500 then went through three rounds with thousands of people and has been oversubscribed. 'We welcome this because ultimately we want to build a deep coaching culture in the company,' Tanuj continued. 'This upskilling enables People Leaders to "pay it forward" in the sense they are investing now in a skill that will become more valuable over time.' It's also enabled the bank to push forward their agenda to broaden their leadership cadre. They are running cohorts across the twenty African states they are represented in, creating opportunities for local talented people to build future valuable skills.

Standard Chartered – questions for reflection
To what extent do you have analytical data on the strengths and development needs of your managers? It would be worthwhile as you go about the redesign of work to take a closer look at the upskill opportunities in place. What is your view of the Standard Chartered focus on coaching skills? Is this an initiative that could have an impact in your company?

<u>Action #13</u>
Act and Create using the pivotal role of good managers

- Consider your narrative of managers in the company. If the assumption is that they are the 'permafrost', is it time to re-evaluate their contribution, to rename and to create a strong community across managers?
- Take a look at the architecture of the role. Would it make sense to split it into those tasks around work scheduling and those that focus on people?
- Do you need to uplift the digital agenda in support of managers? Are you collecting sufficient data and experimenting enough with AI? Have you considered the behavioural nudges that could support managers?
- Are you devoting sufficient resources to upskilling managers in crucial elements such as empathy and coaching?

Act and Create: The power of co-creation

Fundamentally redesigning work will impact on every employee. The pathway of redesign should have real benefits as people have a chance to work in ways that support them to be more productive. Yet, as I've shown, there are hurdles to navigate. How will teams actually work together when some are face to face and others are virtual? How will virtual meetings actually work at times of conflict? What happens when innovation begins to slump and clear changes in work structures have to be made? There is no doubt that well-developed work scheduling combined with line managers who are skilled and empathic will play a key role.

Yet moving into the day-to-day actions that will come with the redesign of work will inevitably rely on employees' goodwill and their capacity to stay open minded about the unavoidable glitches along the way. How can you be sure your colleagues arrive at this positive feeling about the future and with goodwill about the journey?

Employees and the nature of change

The classic approach to managing change is to take the 'top-down' route. Goals and direction, such as 'you will be in the office three days a week', are decided by senior executives and then communicated to employees. This has the advantage of clarity, a unity of purpose (there is only one message) and speed of communication (from one to many). But whilst on the face of it this hoped-for unity and speed have clear advantages, in practice they often fail to deliver on these promises. That's in part because employees are not necessarily bought into the leadership message. Yes – they hear it, but that doesn't mean they act on it. And even if they do, there could be a great deal of passive resistance.

Why might this be the case? It's not a straightforward answer – and it's not the same for all employees or all companies. Of course, it could be that people simply don't understand how the broad message translates into their everyday action – what exactly are they supposed to do tomorrow that's different from today? It might be an issue of capability, for whilst people may understand the message, they don't believe they have the skills or capabilities to make it happen. Take hybrid working, where people might be recruited to the concept, but don't have the capabilities to create complex schedules or manage virtual team meetings.

Underlying all this is the fundamental question we all ask when faced with change – what's in it for me? Will this make me more skilled or better at my job, help me get that pay rise, make me more interesting to others, give me space to have more fun? These are essentially issues of motivation, and if the answer is 'yes' you are more likely to adopt these new actions. In a sense you are propelled into the future because you believe it will be better; you are engaged because you feel positive about the future and about your ability to take on this new challenge.

What of the route to change that uses the 'burning platform' method? Wouldn't it be simpler to say to people, 'You have to do this because the company is about to go bust', or, 'You have to do this and if you don't you will be fired'? My London Business School colleague Constantinos (Costas) Markides asked chief executives whether the following statement was true: 'To create a sense of urgency, you have to make your people appreciate the imminent threat of disruption and the mortal danger the company is facing.' He found 74 per cent agreed. But in his view, nothing could be further from the truth.[3] To create a more 'permanent sense of urgency', Costas suggests, leaders should make the need for change positive and personal, and encourage employees to feel emotionally committed to the necessary transformation.[4] The business strategist John Hagel agrees. He argues that it is true that the Covid-19 conflagration and the smouldering climate emergency are real crises.[5] But leaders can acknowledge the challenges and obstacles of the current volatility, whilst still pointing out the path towards new positive goals. As Hagel told the *Financial Times* columnist Andrew Hill, 'Instead, too often chief executives "just want to hold on to what they have". It's a world of increasing pressure. But it's also a world of expanding opportunity.'[6]

Like Costas and John, I'm also not a fan of the burning platform way of thinking about change – and here's why. As a psychologist, I know that change almost inevitably requires us to stop doing something, perhaps something that we cherish, and to start to do something that's unknown to us, and in which we probably don't have confidence right now. That's why learning as an adult can be so tough. It's not simply about adding something to our repertoire, it's almost inevitably about 'unlearning', dropping something out. And in order to be prepared to let go and unlearn, we need to feel good about ourselves and good about our context. Now imagine that in this redesign of work change you've been presented with the burning platform – either you change or you are in danger of losing your job. How do you feel? Faced with this threat, your brain moves immediately into the 'fight-or-flight' response. Your anxiety increases and you ready yourself to confront or retreat. In this state you are unlikely to learn, and, fundamentally, learning is at the heart of changing.

So, whilst the top-down approach superficially looks the best way to go, and the burning platform has its own attractions, neither is capable of engaging people in the way the redesign of work requires. There are alternatives. The bottom-up approach sounds like a recipe for anarchy as people across the company decide what they want and this percolates up the organization. Yet there is a middle way, one which both acknowledges that the leadership of the organization has views and a strategy and also brings into the mix the ideas, insights and energy of the whole organization. This is the path of co-creation. The challenge is that, like much of the redesign of work, it needs a high degree of intentionality and design thinking.

The power of taking a wider perspective

We looked earlier at how the executive team at Brit reached out into diverse peer groups to co-create ways of working. The shift in the idea of this from being a face-to-face activity to a virtual activity was enabled by collaborative technology. Could this collaborative technology be used to join an even greater number of employees together to co-create new ways of working?

This has been a question that has intrigued me for more than a decade. The initial trigger was my goal to experiment with bringing together executives from the companies who participated in my Future of Work Consortium at HSM Advisory. We had created connectivity between the corporate executives with a series of annual face-to-face events in London, Tokyo, Sydney and New York. And whilst I did not see these face-to-face events disappearing, we wanted to augment them. So we began the process of designing and testing a collaborative platform that would support co-creation. I'd been inspired by my German academic colleagues professors Frank Piller and Kathrin Moeslein. They were collaborating with teams at

MIT led by Henry Chesbrough, and pioneering 'open innovation' in companies from Siemens to Volkswagen.[7] From them I'd learnt that, whilst the technology of the platform is important, it's in the process of facilitation and the flow of conversations that the real value is added.

With that in mind we started to build collaborative platforms with the aim of supporting companies in their quest for co-creation. My colleague Harriet Molyneaux was particularly fascinated by how this could widen the conversation about values. What we learnt along the way became the foundation of the practice we now use to support companies in enabling their employees to co-create new ways of working.

Insight: How Ericsson enables meaningful conversations

Bringing employees along was a crucial part of the process of change for Ericsson, the Swedish technology multinational head-quartered in Stockholm with expertise in 5G and the Internet of Things (IoT). In 2017 the new CEO, Börje Ekholm, talked with his leadership team about the challenges they faced in a tough business climate and a company that was delivering poor results. As Selina Millstam, who is the vice president and head of talent management, told me, 'We decided to do more in a true co-created way. We wanted to harness the collective intelligence and see, from a pragmatic perspective, where things were working well and not well.' The starting point was asking tough questions and having meaningful conversations. To support this, Selina and her team designed a three-day programme which they quickly rolled out to groups of 100: 'It was very much employee led; we wanted to break down the hierarchies and encourage people to learn from each other regardless of their level. I positioned this as an experiment – I couldn't guarantee it was going to work.'

Over the following years this initial intervention did much to connect the various businesses and had gone some way towards democratizing information and ideas. Then, as the senior team began to look more deeply at new ways of working, they agreed that a guiding principle would be that every new work arrangement would have to be rooted in Ericsson's company culture and values. Important aspects of the culture were 'a speak-up environment', 'empathy' and 'cooperation and collaboration'.

OPENING UP THE CONVERSATION TO EVERYONE

By 2019 they decided to open the conversation about ways of working to everyone in the company. As Selina remarked:

> Inviting everyone was a big step, it was a real gesture of inclusion. It was around creating a voice and democratizing this whole initiative. We wanted to unpack what our values meant and look at the behaviours – to demystify conversations. For most employees there is a sense that they aren't included – but here we invited everyone in to talk about how we work together and what our processes look like. There is something very fundamentally human around this – about being heard and contributing.

In the first of a series of conversations, 3,750 leaders and managers conversed over a 75-hour period about the future and values of the company. By 2020 the plan was to broaden the conversation to discuss the new working arrangements and how the potential new ways of working might affect Ericsson's culture. All 95,000 employees from across the world were invited to engage in an in-the-moment, moderated conversation. So on 28 April, just two months into the pandemic, more than 17,000 people participated in this virtual conversation. They created more than 28,000 conversational threads which addressed issues such as how working during the pandemic had created both challenges (such as lack of social contact) and benefits (such as increased productivity through reduced distraction).

This created a shared sense of the collective destiny of Ericsson. As Selina told me at the time, 'All the members of the executive team and a significant percentage of the executive population came into the conversation.' That meant, for example, someone in an administration role could have a real-time, unfiltered conversation with the CEO, or a software developer in India could talk at length to a customer relations person in Germany. As Selina said, 'There was something raw and authentic about listening to people speak and contemplate in the moment.'

Selina and I have reflected on how this process of co-creation has supported the redesign of work and aligned this with the values of the corporation. Her view was that it increased people's 'peripheral awareness'. It allowed and encouraged people to hear from others outside their immediate circle. That's crucial to get over some of the issues of in-groups and out-groups that can lead to disharmony. By listening to others, people had a chance to be more understanding and empathic of their situation.

An important feature of the process was the teams of facilitators who engaged and supported those on the platform to have a much wider conversation. The facilitators did this by giving people confidence to speak out – using phrases such as 'Could you tell me more about this?' or 'That sounds interesting – do you have an example of how this worked for you?' This gave people courage to speak out. The facilitators also engineered new encounters by connecting people who were following a similar conversational thread – such as 'There is a person in another country / business, etc., who is also talking about this – let me connect you.'

This process of co-creation has shaped how people at Ericsson are thinking about the redesign of work in a number of ways. It engaged people directly in the conversation, so everyone who got involved had a better idea of what others felt, the choices and trade-offs they faced and how this measured up to their own experience. As Selina reflected, 'People could empathize with each other as they listened to and shared their own stories. And from a process perspective, it brought to light the many experiments and workarounds that were taking place across the company.' That gave Selina a chance to survey these experiments, to identify those champions who really cared about these experiments, and by doing so bring together groups of people committed to pushing these ideas forward.

LESSONS FROM ERICSSON'S OPENING OF THE CONVERSATION

My advisory group HSM Advisory have used this collaborative process in many of the companies we have been supporting as they use co-creational processes to redesign work. I asked Graham Oxley and Harriet Molyneaux what we had learnt. They point to four key learnings:

> First, we've learnt that support from leaders is crucial. Leaders need a chance to scope the goal of the co-creation process. That's why we begin with a series of executive workshops to understand more deeply the scope of the questions leaders want to address and the broad areas they are interested in. The benefit is that this builds commitment within the executive team and ensures they are active participants in what results.
>
> Second, along the way we've learnt that bringing what can be hundreds of thousands of people onto the platform is a significant communication and engagement effort. So we've devised a whole array of ways to entice people to join the conversation. Importantly, during the typically three days of online collaborative conversations, trained facilitators play a crucial role in steering the conversation to cover all the topics that the executive team are interested in, as well as pulling out new ideas and insights.
>
> Third, when it comes to analysing the conversation threads, we've discovered that what works best in analysing the qualitative data is augmentation between human and machines. So, whilst the team use an AI program for sentiment analysis and to show the network connections between people (for example, who replied to whom), we've found that human 'eyeballing the data' is crucial. Finding the threads of insights, pulling out the crucial themes and

seeing how this aligns with culture and values is the task of a skilled human.

Fourth, as in any process of co-creation, when executives actively ask employees for their insights and opinions, it's crucial they act on what they hear. That's why, following the three-day virtual conversation we typically bring together those 'champions' who have been particularly interested in a topic to form groups to push these ideas forward.

Ericsson – questions for reflection
Consider how the team at Ericsson went about the redesign of work. Are there ways that you could build a wider perspective and bring people from across the organization together to discuss the redesign of work? Do you have any experience of facilitated online platforms like the one that Ericsson is using and, if not, are there aspects of the learnings about these large-scale conversations that you could bring into your own company?

Action #14
Act and Create using the power of co-creation

- Consider the means by which you have until now steered the process of change. What have been the advantages and disadvantages?
- Take a look at the process of co-creation you have in place. How is it working for you?
- Experiment by taking an aspect of the model of the redesign of work and running it through a co-creation process. What have you learnt from this experience?

Act and Create: The leader's narrative

Leaders can play a central role in supporting the redesign of work by working with others to develop the goals and principles that frame the redesign, by creating a sense of experimentation and excitement so people feel able to try out new ideas and believe it is OK to fail, and by role-modelling the behaviours that will be crucial to how work gets done.

Yet beyond all these important roles, when it comes to redesigning work, what most fascinates me is the role of leader as narrator. By that I mean how the leadership team describe the future: the words they use, the stories they tell, the pictures they create in the minds of others. It seems to me that in those times when your company is in the period of 'unfreeze', when so much is up for grabs and there is anxiety about how things will play out, these narratives are pivotal.

In part that's because your business is an incredibly complex social structure, framed by practices and processes that establish the daily rhythm of work, connected by invisible networks through which knowledge flows and inhabited by groups of people who may or may not trust or like each other.

If you are a leader then you are required to in a sense 'hold' this system in your mind and then describe it to yourself and to others. At the same time you need to be looking outside the company – at what your competitors are doing, at your partnerships and stake-holders, at how the financial markets are responding and at what customers and advocacy groups are saying. You will inevitably be party to powerful forces and dynamics. Being a leader is a tough job. The very best leaders behave in an authentic way and are able, even under conditions of stress and strain, to reach into their values to make the day-to-day judgements that frame their lives. Import-antly, they are also empathic to others – listening to their concerns, understanding their challenges. It is their narrative that will play a crucial role in how the redesign of work becomes actioned and how it is created.

The nature of narratives

Companies are full of stories or narratives, which are the all-pervasive building blocks of corporate identity, featured in the history of the company posted on its website and in the stories and gossip about it that people share. Employees use this information to make sense of their experiences and create a view of what it is to be part of the organization.

These stories play an especially crucial role during 'unfreeze', times of change and flux, when people could be anxious and fearful. When people hear stories about the future, about what might be, this helps them make sense of time and of causality. And because these stories are collective experiences, they help groups frame their experiences and build and solidify their collective identity.

The impact stories have on us has been revealed by neuroscientists through a series of studies.[8] They discovered that narrative and stories build connections between the storyteller and listener. And when examining the brain patterns created whilst people are listening to stories, they found increasing activity and connectivity in the left temporal cortex – the area of the brain where emotions, memories and speech are processed. Interestingly, these neural changes last beyond the period of the experiment, for several days. Hearing data and facts (rather than stories and narratives) does not activate the same neural pathways.

As work is redesigned, so narratives are reshaped. Stewart Friedman, a professor at the Wharton School of the University of Pennsylvania, has been studying leadership for decades.[9] His view is clear – great leaders are 'real' in the sense that others know what they care about. As he coaches leaders he encourages them to learn to tell inspiring stories about who they are and where they are going. As he says: 'When we know our stories, we know ourselves.' For him, the strongest narratives are compelling stories of an achievable future. They compel by engaging and capturing the heart and use images that help others create concrete visualizations – people can imagine themselves in this future. And they are achievable, for although they are in the future, they are not so far away that it's out of reach.

In Stewart's view the pandemic created an even greater opportunity for narrative:

> We all compose stories about our history and our future. When leaders talk about where they come from it shows them in the context of their own development. People want to hear about their lives beyond their work role – during the pandemic they often shared the demands and joys of life beyond work. Sharing their role as a parent or friend creates a sense of willingness to share.

During the pandemic Stewart saw great leaders opening with a simple question: 'How are you feeling these days?' As he told me: 'Questions like this give people an opportunity to express – from gratitude to grief – it's these small things that change the nature of the relationship and shift the conversation from instrumental to one of common humanity.'

He also saw real opportunities for leaders to support and engage in experimentation – trying something new, learning, adjusting. This is an opportunity, as he told me, when 'the power of language can push people past their natural fear and anxiety. They can become more open to imagine a different future. Perhaps this is the moment when work–life is less about balance and more a continuously creative negotiation about mutual gain.' That is why how leaders talk about this future and the way they role model through their own behaviour will play a crucial role in the redesign of work.

Leaders in their own words

I'm fortunate to have had two great leaders, Ann Cairns and Mervyn Davies, teach with me for over four years on my Future of

Work elective at the London Business School. Both use this teaching opportunity to discuss with my MBA students their leadership journey, their broader view of how leadership has changed in their lifetime, and how they expect it to change looking forward. They also share their own narratives with us.

Ann is deputy chairman of Mastercard. She also chairs both the executive group that supports the UK government department on business and innovation (BAIS) and the Thirty Per Cent Group, which works across the world to increase the representation of women on boards. Hers is a path of experience that has taken her from being an engineer on an oil rig to an investment banker at Citibank responsible in part for the reconstruction of Lehman Brothers following its collapse in 2008, to her present leadership position with Mastercard. My students have great admiration for her, and she is an important role model for everyone in the class. Here are some of the highlights from her conversations with my students on 26 May 2021:

> In my view leadership comes down to values. There are many moments of truth when I'm taking a decision and people are reacting. They are judging me by asking themselves, 'Is this a decent person?' I want to be honest with myself and with them and it takes courage and tenacity to ask the tough questions.
>
> As a leader, I don't want too much stability – I want to encourage myself and others to be energetic and to take initiatives. It's important to never be afraid of change.
>
> When I joined Mastercard it was a smaller company and it's grown rapidly. Yet it is important we keep it as flat as possible without allowing hierarchy to creep in. The connections are important and as a leader I want to be accessible – I want to be an 'ordinary person' whom my colleagues can relate to. I want to be empathic to their situation.

Mervyn Davies served as the CEO and then chairman of Standard Chartered bank. He later became the Minister for Business in the UK government and now sits in the House of Lords. He's also a serial entrepreneur and the chair of several financial and cultural institutions. Here is his narrative from 19 May 2021:

> This is a profound time – tensions between countries, the impact of the pandemic, monetary policy, inflation, climate change, growing inequality. This is an era of consumer activism – the pace of change is extraordinary.
>
> As a leader I have to take a view – on our ESG [environmental, social, and governance] goals, on corporate tax, on what we deliver. I'm judged on financial goals such as earning per share. But it's more than this. What is the purpose of the corporation? Are we a good company? That can mean taking a view on tough calls around, for example, minimum wage or the use of plastics. I want to think more broadly beyond judging the business by economic success – to think beyond GDP.
>
> My attitudes to change matter. I need to make judgement calls about work–life balance, about the career choices I make, the holidays I take and how I spend time with my family.

These are two leaders talking about their leadership journey, what they believe in and how they narrate this. Others, of course, will have their own perspective and journey. What I wanted to illustrate is that they have a great deal on their mind and a great deal to consider.

How the best leaders narrate their stories

It seems to me that one of the challenges we face – either as a leader or, like me, as an observer, is that in organizations it's easy to get carried away with the machinery: to talk about practices and processes, about 'agile', or the reward processes, or the new chatbot or the AI system. It's not that this machinery is not important. It is important – but it's not what motivates people. Talking about data does not activate the emotional part of our brains. That's the stuff that goes on inside the engine. What we humans are excited by is the bigger stuff – the stories, and preferably stories about people. That's why in Chapter 2 I made the suggestion of using 'personas' as a way of creating a framework for people to answer the question 'What does the redesign of work mean for this person, in this situation, at this time of their life?'

The press abounds with narratives as leaders try to make sense of what is happening now and create a narrative of the future. Here is an example: a CEO says, 'I want everyone back in the office five days a week.' They are talking about the future and as soon as they say it, people are beginning to imagine what this means for them. The listeners are trying to make sense of their own and their collective future. As they think about this narrative, what is the sense they will make of it? What is this narrative telling them?

It's essentially a message that is binary in that there are two choices: office or home. It has a finality about it – this is how it will be. And, importantly for the listener, it's a message that implicitly conveys a top-down approach. It's got a whiff – to use psychological speak – of a parent–child relationship, with the leader parent 'knowing best' what the employee child needs. How will people respond to this? My guess is that some will buy into the message, whilst others will resist it. What might an alternative narrative look like? Right now, in this time of uncertainty, that's not straightforward. But here are some ideas.

On the issue of binary choice, the leader could widen the scope and acknowledge that we are in a time of extraordinary transition when there is a chance to rethink assumptions. It is a time to rethink assumptions about place and rethink assumptions about time. A moment to be creative, imaginative and bold.

On the finality of the message, the leader could acknowledge that this period of 'unfreeze' is a time for experiments and prototypes, an opportunity for options to be modelled and tested. It is also a moment to speak of the purpose and values of the business and how these values can create, in a sense, the 'guard rails' for action.

On the top-down approach, the leader could use this opportunity to commit to widening the conversation and to move to co-creation where they are part of the conversation rather than a sole voice. To admit that they don't know all the answers and to invite others to contribute.

These narratives become hollow rhetoric unless they are supported by everyday actions. When Mastercard's Ann Cairns speaks of 'moments of truth' it is this she is acknowledging. She is commenting on the universal fact that leaders are watched with a great deal of interest by others. The credibility of their words and narratives are constantly tested against their actual behaviour. Does the reality match up to the rhetoric? But it is not simply watching – it's also acting. A leader's day-to-day behaviour implicitly impacts on how others behave through the process of imitation. Imitation is how humans learn, and the more powerful the people, the more likely they are to be imitated.

What are the leadership behaviours and actions that could make a significant difference to redesigning work? It seems to me that key will be their behaviour around flexibility and autonomy, around co-creation and about being innovative and experimental.

In many companies a redesign principle has been to attempt to create flexibility and autonomy around time and place. The benefits are obvious – people are less stressed, more likely to positively engage with work, less likely to leave.

In order to get a sense of whether these redesign principles are rhetoric or reality, employees look to the everyday behaviour of leaders – to the 'moments of truth'. Do they, like Mervyn Davies earlier, talk about their family and the way they are thinking about their own work–life balance? Do they acknowledge the challenges they face and describe how they are approaching these challenges?

Leaders' behaviours and preferences about top-down versus co-creation are also highly visible. Do leaders go out of their way to listen to others? And *who* do they listen to? Mervyn, for example, during his time in leadership positions at Standard Chartered, was famous for sending texts to hundreds of people across the whole company. As he explained to me:

I want to listen to everyone – from the receptionist in the Mumbai office to the FX dealers in Hong Kong. That means walking around and talking with people. And I supported this by creating groups whom I would send texts to simply asking 'How's it going?' – checking in with them. I wanted to listen to what was happening to them.

Today, of course, it's possible with Zoom and other collaborative platforms to reach out to hundreds of thousands of people simultaneously. I asked Selina Millstam of Ericsson about the impact leadership involvement had during the company's three-day, moderated conversation discussed earlier:

During the seventy-two-hour period of being online across the whole community there was great excitement and activity when the CEO Börje Ekholm and his team came into the conversation. It's unusual to have a 'raw', unscripted conversation with a senior leader and people wanted to talk about a range of issues. In these encounters the CEO responded in the moment, without their office or communications team on hand – it was incredibly authentic.

Finally, beyond the rhetoric of innovation – does the leader actually try things out and experiment? What do they do when others fail?

When Stewart Friedman studied leaders he saw this capacity to be innovative and act with creativity as crucial. In his view leaders should be prepared to design experiments, to work out what works.

Action #15
Act and Create using the leader narrative

- What are the current leadership narratives? What message are they conveying?

- Think about the core aspects of the redesign of work. Which are the most significant?
- What are the stories that leaders can tell that link to these core aspects whilst reflecting their own interests and values?

Act and Create: The four steps of redesigning work

Redesigning a company can seem overwhelming. As I've worked with my advisory group HSM Advisory to support a variety of companies on their journey, I've discovered that, whilst all four stages of redesigning work are important to experience, the outcome – the signature – is unique.

It is now your mission to create your signature – and to do that you need to bring all the frames, insights and reflections together. To give you a sense of the total cycle of activity, I want to share how the executive team in one company went about it. My advisory group and I have been advising the executive team at accounting-software providers Sage about how best to redesign work and how to embark on the four steps. You will see how they approached each of them and discover the lessons they learnt.

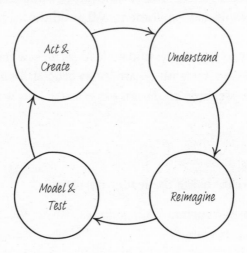

The strategic context and purpose

First, some context. For the leadership team at Sage, the pandemic came at a time when they were already engaged in a business transformation. Founded in 1981 to computerize accounting payroll and human capital management (HCM) processes, Sage had developed into the global market leader in the back-office digital transformation of small and medium-sized businesses. By 2021 it employed around 13,000 people and had significantly widened its footprint, serving over two million customers in twenty countries in Europe, America, Africa and Australia.

In late 2018 the leadership team, led by CEO Steve Hare, began to shift the business model from traditional on-premises software to cloud-based software as a service (SaaS), with a strong emphasis on technology and the customer journey. This strategic transition had profound implications on the valued capabilities within the company. In the traditional business model, the sales force and sales support team play a key role in building close relationships with customers – either speaking to them regularly on the phone or travelling to meet them on site and then working closely to ensure customers repeat their purchase. In a SaaS business model it's digital skills that come to the fore, with roles such as digital marketing taking centre stage as the business moves from a sales cycle to a customer cycle. To make this switch the leadership team had begun to redefine the customer journey and reposition the workflows to better execute and deliver the new customer experience.

The impact of the pandemic was to speed up this strategic transition whilst also creating an opportunity to design a way of working that would be enticing for people with these hard-to-find and valuable digital skills. I spoke with Aoife Fitzmaurice, who heads up Sage's Workplace Futures programme, about those early months of the pandemic:

It was crisis management, we needed to move 13,000 colleagues to fully virtual and maintain services in twenty global locations. But it was a real proof point – we realized we could operate effectively virtually. Without the nudge of the pandemic we would not have thought this was possible – the proof was in the experience.

The leadership team saw this as an opportunity to think deeply about what they had learnt from the pandemic and how they wanted people to 'show up'. The business mission of Sage is to 'remove barriers by transforming the way people think and work, so everyone has an opportunity to thrive'. The collective experiences of the pandemic gave the leadership team an opportunity to reflect this mission to 'remove barriers' both with their customers, and also with their employees.

Step 1: Understand

The opportunity for Sage was to transform work in ways that would be iconic and create a compelling employee proposition for talented people both within the company and for potential new recruits. To do that, Aoife and her colleagues convened a design team, which began in March 2020 to communicate this initiative and then ran a series of virtual workshops to understand more deeply the needs and aspirations of employees. This was an important first step. As Aoife told me:

When we started to build the case for change we wanted to take a data driven approach. So we started with our internal data, looking at difference sources including performance data and the 'always listening' and quarterly 'pulse' surveys that provide rich colleague insights including ENPS (Employee Net Promoter Score). Comparing pre-pandemic data from those 10 per cent of the population working from home with office-based workers, we were able to identify some trends. For example, we found that those working from home in some cases had higher ENPS scores. Our experience of working more flexibly was that colleagues felt more productive. There was also great goodwill and empathy with each other to make this work in the longer term.

The design team then complemented this baselining data by examining industry trends, particularly in the technology sector. This analysis strongly reinforced the case for change.

The design team made this data-driven case for change to the leadership team, including Steve Hare and Amanda Cusdin, the chief people officer, to review and consider. They set out the problem statement and working hypothesis and asked the leadership team 'How do we want to show up?' and 'How does this link to our purpose?'

Step 2: Reimagine

Then they began to reimagine. It was clear that employees' expectations were heightened by their experience of the pandemic, as evidenced in the survey data, and they wanted to have a voice in the redesign of work.

To widen this perspective the design team embarked on co-creating with 200 employees from across the whole business. Mirroring the experience of the leadership team, they made an upfront investment in setting out the 'forward focus' – sharing the trends that would shape their industry and looking at what other companies were doing.

Then, using this forward focus, in a series of design sessions they continued the co-creation by asking people to reimagine work in the future. They explored a number of themes – how work could be redesigned so as to maintain personal boundaries; what it would take to design work in a way that established fairness, and what the viable options for home / office working were. From this an initial model for flexible working was drafted which could be discussed and tested more broadly.

Looking back to these design sessions Aoife reflects:

People really understood the issues of flexibility around place – they understood the issues of working from home and the office and the implications on connections and collaboration. As they looked across the company it was clear that flexibility in terms of time when it was used was often inconsistent. This inconsistency created the potential for people to see it as unfair.

With this in mind the team explored how other companies were approaching time flexibility in ways that were consistent and fair.

GETTING EXECUTIVE BUY-IN

This initial model was then taken to the leadership team in two design sessions. These were tough sessions as executives pushed back and tested the thinking about time and place. Yet looking back, these sessions proved to be instrumental in gaining leadership buy-in and in refining the 'red lines' of the principles that would shape how choices were made.

Following this a cross-functional team, the 'future working group' (including people from internal communications, customer and colleague experience, technology and talent acquisition), began to map the impact on the employee journey. A particular focus was to understand how the new ways of working could be enhanced by technology and process improvements.

AGREEING THE FOUR GUIDING PRINCIPLES

Four guiding principles were agreed in order to drive a consistent approach to making choices in this new model – customer centric, fairness and trust, human connection, experimentation. For each principle, non-negotiable 'red lines' were established that reinforced some of the unchanging aspects of the model.

The first principle was that any model of work had to maintain or increase *customer centric performance*. So a crucial 'red line' was that the redesign would focus on outcomes and adapt to meet changing customer needs.

The next principle was *fairness and trust*, and a non-negotiable 'red line' was that flexible working would not be a reward but rather rooted in the trust of employees, and trade-offs would require everyone to compromise and be accountable.

Then, the redesign of work would be capable of strengthening rather than depleting *human connections*. Intentional and purposeful communication patterns would be crucial in changing workflows. Any design had to support the human connection and the sense of inclusion that had developed in the previous eighteen months.

And finally, in the rollout of these new working practices, employees would be encouraged to engage in *courageous experimentation* and to take risks. As Aoife explained, 'This final principle was really important. There was nervousness in the system that we would make the wrong choice. So it was crucial that people felt they could be bold and courageous.' So, for example, new team agreements on flexible working would be tried, reflected on and then adapted. There was a growing realization that it would be impossible to get it right first time.

This spirit of experimentation was reflected in the idea that any model had to be tailored to the different parts of the business. What worked for the sales force, for example, might not work for the finance teams. To do this, the focus on *team agreements* provided an opportunity to understand how work gets done in a particular setting whilst creating shared learning across the business.

Step 3: Model and Test

MODELLING THE ARCHETYPES

As the design process built through 2021, the team began to model and describe four archetypal working patterns or modes – homeworkers, flex workers, field workers and office workers.

Homeworkers would be fully remote workers who would be required to come into a Sage office only if there arose a business need. This would include occasional face-to-face collaboration days with colleagues. It was likely homeworkers would make up about 10 per cent of the employee base.

Flex workers would work both at home and in the office. In the past there had been some informal flexible working agreements, now the aim was to bring these conversations to all the teams. For flex workers, the 'sweet spot' of in-office collaboration days was discussed within the team and then agreed with the manager. This 'sweet spot' could range from one to five days a week in the office. When in the office, flex workers could book a workstation in team 'villages', whilst team agreements set out the ground rules for face-to-face collaboration days.

The two other working models, both comprising relatively small percentages of the total workforce, were *field workers*, in roles that require face-to-face customer contact, and *office workers*, who needed to be in the office full time with a personally allocated workstation.

BEING BOLD

Beyond the flex on place, the leadership team wanted to be bold and experimental and push out the frontiers of what was possible even further. One such experiment was *work away*, a geographically flexible option in which employees would have the chance to relocate to another work location for up to ten weeks. This option was a response to insights about the workforce, many of whom had family in other countries, and some of whom really enjoyed travelling. As Aoife remarked, 'We realized this could be a point of differentiation in a very competitive talent field. Some of the people we really need are attracted to being "digital nomads"; we wanted to give them the opportunity to do this.'

Step 4: Act and Create

Finally, Sage had to act and create. The design team took several creative actions, four of which are detailed here.

CREATE A MANAGERIAL 'PLAYBOOK'

As the work model was finalized, groups of managers in a series of workshops tested the experience and from these a managerial 'playbook' was developed, much as in the case of Brit Insurance in Chapter 4. The aspiration here was, rather than being bureaucratic and highly centralized, to be 'light touch' in showing managers how to create team agreement, how to bring a team together and how to focus on deliverables and outcomes. Into this was woven insights that would help them – about networks and knowledge flows, the nature of boundaries and how well-being is maintained.

SCALE UP LEADERSHIP DESIGN CAPABILITY

Then there was a push to dramatically scale up leadership engagement and buy-in. It was acknowledged that going forward, these new models of work would only be successful if leaders were confident and convinced these new ways of working would support rather than detract from customer focus. To do this a series of *talking points* were developed that leaders could use as they told their own narratives and stories. These talking points described reasons why employees should be excited by this, the positive impact on talent attraction and retention, the way these new ways of working would support the strategic aim of the software as a service, and what the best tech companies do. The leadership narrative was clear: this was not simply about flex, and it was not a 'race to the bottom' – this was a tool to increase performance and improve employee experience. And, importantly, this was something leaders were choosing to do rather than being told to do.

Together the managers' playbook and the leaders' talking points served as a guide to action. They would ensure managers and leaders understood the choices their teams faced. And, crucially, it would support them to navigate the move to flexible work in a fair and equitable way whilst strengthening social connections. As one executive explained, 'We did not want a top-down approach – but we did want fairness across the teams. We saw it as a process of experimentation, testing out new ways of working, then learning from our experience and course correcting.'

DEVELOP TEAM-LEVEL AGREEMENTS

The flex model was actioned as managers set about agreeing with their team members how best to flex work within the whole team. They began by creating a team agreement that described the ground rules. Using a design session with their team, they began by defining the sweet spot of when the team would be cooperating in the office and when they would be collaborating or engaging in focused work at home. Over time, and as each manager spoke with their own management peers in other parts of the business, it became clear that the timing of these sweet spots was different across the teams. So, as managers communicated with their peers and received feedback from their own team members, the whole management community began to learn more about how to be flexible and customer centric. The finance team, for example, had begun by agreeing to be in the office together four days a week, but rapidly learnt that in fact three days was optimal. For other teams that were globally dispersed, being together face to face was always considered a crucial but infrequent activity. So, learning from the pandemic experience and the enhanced digital capability, they set about designing work more intentionally, with a strong synchronous virtual element coupled with occasional face-to-face meetings.

LEARN AND ITERATE

Whilst there was broad agreement about how choices about place could be made that would strengthen human connection, there was a realization that when it came to flexibility of time, more design thought and intentionality would be needed. As Aoife said, 'We quickly understood place, but there was more uncertainty about how to design for flexibility of time.' To deepen understanding a series of pilots around flexing time was launched, with a focus on work scheduling practices and the best way to use technology to create an objective assessment of the appropriateness of flexibility for each role. To do this a methodology was developed that enabled an objective 'flex score' to be created by role and team, indicating the potential for time and place flexibility. Could a role, for example, be performed by a homeworker or as part of a job-share, or on a part-time basis? Another experiment was aimed at promoting more job-shares in senior roles, starting by redesigning a senior job-share with a view to learning from this and then scaling across the organization.

I spoke with the design team in the summer of 2021 when they were very much in the acting and creating phase. As Aoife reflected, 'We are experimenting and learning – we are really only at the start.' I also asked Dr Anna Gurun, who led the project for HSM Advisory, what she had learnt. She pointed to three aspects:

First, framing the approach around guiding principles (rather than rules) meant people felt a sense of collective purpose without it being too restrictive or inflexible in telling people *how* to work. Second, the commitments and red lines showed people that the organization was firm in making sure certain elements would remain, even if other aspects changed or evolved. Third, involving people in crafting the behaviours needed to work effectively meant that they were grounded in the way people worked rather than being top-down led.

I was interested in what the Sage team anticipated as the benefits from this complex process of negotiation and learning. They pointed to the business mission of Sage – to knock down barriers so everyone can thrive. They realized that to do this they needed to create an inclusive workplace that would attract and retain the best talent. They acknowledged the design process was lengthy, but they believe it was the best chance they had to design work that enables people to thrive at a place and time they choose.

Action #16
Act and Create using the four steps of redesigning work

- Take a look at the four steps. Where are you now on the journey? Are there steps you need to re-evaluate or engage with in a more purposeful manner? What is the sequence you have gone through?
- With your design colleagues take a look at the way that the team at Sage approached the redesign of work. What resonates most with you? Are there aspects that would not work in your company? Why would that be?
- Consider the various ways the design team at Sage created engagement with the design process – from employees, managers, executives and the senior team. Are there any aspects to this that would resonate with your own company?
- As you reflect on the questions following each design stage, what is your biggest priority right now? What are the actions you could engage with that would make the most significant contribution to creating your unique signature model of work?

The Way Forward

This is your chance to redesign work to ensure it is fit for purpose for the coming decades. You have an opportunity to learn from our collective experience and imagination, and from the journey we are all going on. This is a time for leaders to step up and positively build from this pandemic experience. To harness new-found digital skills, to continue to push to dismantle bureaucracy and to create flexibility for many. This is also a time to confront issues that have been on the table for the last decade but which we have not been able to solve – such as the reality that being 'always on' is tough and that human networks and connections, though often invisible, really matter.

In this book I have set out a way to redesign work – to ask the crucial questions, to engage in the four-step process and to articulate your company's 'signature' characteristics. My view is that, whilst looking at 'best practice' is useful to broaden your imagination, ultimately each one of us and our organization has to find a way that uniquely reflects our own purpose, context and capabilities.

To help you navigate this I have brought insights from organizations from across the world and in many different sectors. My hope is that you have also engaged with the reflective questions that follow each corporate insight to bring these learnings into your own organization and situation. I have also drawn from a range of frameworks that can help you bring structure and form to your ideas and conversations.

So now is the time to jump into action. Here is what I would put on your to-do list.

Create a cross-functional design team

When HSM Advisory supports companies to redesign work, our initial suggestion is they begin by pulling together a multifunctional design team. The members should ideally represent the functional areas of capabilities within the organization who will play a significant part in implementation. In most cases you will want representation from human resources to consider mobility, rewards and performance management. In some design teams – such as HSBC – the marketing function played an important role. And in most design teams there is representation from the technology and the business strategy function.

It is this team who will then engage on the four steps.

However, you might also, like the executives at Brit Insurance, go beyond the 'usual suspects' to bring in the voices of people from across the company. Recall that Brit began their design process by creating peer groups that traversed the company – from receptionists to analysts and managing directors. This breadth of engagement brought real momentum to the projects that followed.

You might also want to consider doing what many of our clients have done, and engage a significant proportion of the workforce in a conversation about the redesign of work. Take a closer look at how the team at Ericsson went about this to get a sense of how this works in practice.

Engage with the 'Redesigning Work Playbook'

Once you have your team assembled, it is time to embark on the four-step redesign process. My suggestion is that everyone in the design team read this book, so that you are all acquainted with the frameworks that will support you to create a shared narrative of how you redesign work. It is also useful if you are all aware of the organizational insights and the questions for reflection. My assumption is that over the coming years more organizational and research insights will be developed. I will be following these and you can keep abreast of my observations through my website, www. lyndagratton.com.

To support you in redesigning work I've created a 'Redesigning Work Playbook'. This is a resource that you can use to guide your journey throughout this book and ensure you stay on track. You can download this now at www.hsm-advisory.com/redesigning-work. You will also find a variety of other resources to support you on this exciting journey.

Become part of a Redesigning Work *learning community*

I believe that when it comes to organization learning, insight from peers in other companies is crucial. That's why I launched the Future of Work Consortium more than a decade ago. My aspiration was to bring together executives and researchers to make them aware of the forces that are shaping work and how best to respond to them. It has been this consortium group of executives that has steered much of my own thinking as we all responded to the challenges and the opportunities of the pandemic. You can find out more about this consortium at www.hsm-advisory.com/redesigning-work.

As part of my support to companies, my advisory team created an action-based programme that works with organizations to support managers on how to redesign work. Go to our website to learn more about what this is, and how it works. In joining it, you would become part of a learning community that is dedicated to redesigning work.

These are extraordinary transformational times. We face real challenges, yet also real opportunities. We have a chance now to fundamentally change our relationship to the work we do, to our colleagues and to our organizations. We will transform this relationship by redesigning work. The four steps I have shared with you are an invitation to this transformational journey. There is no doubt there will be obstacles along the way and that our courage and taste for experimentation will be tested. Yet as I look at how people around the world are stepping up to debate, cooperate and build, I am convinced that we can create a future that will support us in being not only more productive in our work but also more fulfilled.

Acknowledgements

Teaching, writing and talking about how work might and could change has been my focus for decades. The impact of the pandemic was that many others shared my passion as we thought how best to use this extraordinary opportunity to transform work in a way we had always hoped to do.

It's this passion that drives the team at my advisory group HSM Advisory, who have performed a sterling job supporting our clients and along the way learnt ever more about how work gets re-designed. Appreciation and gratitude to Harriet Molyneaux, who leads the advisory group, to Emma Birchall, who was an important part of this book, and to Sally McNamara, who heads up our Asian practice. The cornerstone of this research has been the Future of Work Consortium – thank you to Dr Anna Gurun, Sam McCarthy, Graham Oxley and Oliver Ferriman for leading this and the related advisory work. Thank you also to Charlotte Jenkins for doing a great job managing the webinars and my social media.

The story began more than a decade ago when the executives from twenty companies got together to think and talk about work. Since then more than ninety companies have been members of the consortium and I'm deeply appreciative of all the executives who have engaged with us. A special thanks to those members who agreed to be interviewed for the book – Ramkumar Chandrasekaran and Anshoo Kapoor from TCS, Hiroki Hiramatsu from Fujitsu, Nicola Millard from BT and Chris Lamb from the Australian New South Wales Public Commission.

Redesigning work is a complex journey and I am very appreciative of the executive teams who partnered with HSM Advisory on their journey. Some shared their stories and insights – thank you to Dario Kosarac of CPP Investments, Jenni Emery and Joe Correnza from Arup, Aoife Fitzmaurice from Sage, Matthew Wilson and Lorraine Denny from Brit Insurance, Selina Millstam from Ericsson, and Leanne Cutts from HSBC.

My last two books, *The 100-Year Life* and *The New Long Life*, were both co-authored with my London Business School colleague Andrew J. Scott. Andrew is now focusing on longevity, but remains very much part of my intellectual life and someone with whom I can have long and fascinating conversations. Thank you.

On the first day of the pandemic – which for me was 14 March 2020 – I was attending a (virtual) meeting of the World Economic Forum's Future Council on Work, Wages and Job Creation. I co-chair this with Sharan Burrow, who is the General Secretary of the International Trade Union Confederation. As the council met over the following months we were able to share ideas and talk through some of the tough issues we saw emerging. I learnt a great deal from the council members and am very grateful for their dedication to the council and its aspirations.

These have been fascinating times, and I've reached out to many people to hear how they were seeing work and what they were experiencing. I am particularly appreciative of those who contributed to the book: Anne Sheehan from Vodafone, Peter Brown from PwC, Alexandru Dinca, Morag Lynagh and Placid Jover from Unilever, Alex Badenoch from Telstra, Mark Atkinson from Mursion and Tanuj Kapilashrami from Standard Chartered, Michael Sunderman from Verizon and Portia Wu from Microsoft.

As the pandemic developed, my journals became full of impromptu conversations about what others saw or felt – thank you to Kevin Delaney from Reset Work, Andrew Hill from the *FT*, Diane Gherson, Stewart Friedman and my London Business School colleagues Herminia Ibarra and Aneeta Rattan.

Developing a Future of Work elective for the London Business School MBA class was a real thrill. It also give me an opportunity to test out ideas and listen to how my students are thinking about their own future of work. A big thank you to those students, and also to the amazing leaders who have shared their stories with them – Christy Johnson of Artemis Connection, Ann Cairns of Mastercard and Lord Mervyn Davies.

The genesis of this book was a series of columns for MIT's *Sloan Management Review* and an article in the *Harvard Business Review* on hybrid work. My editors at both publications provided incredible support as I honed my ideas and worked through the ideas I wanted to bring. I am very grateful to Toby Lester at *Harvard Business Review*, and especially so to Leslie Brokaw from *MIT Sloan Management Review*, who not only did a sterling job editing my columns but also helped me think through this book.

My editor at Penguin, Lydia Yadi, spotted the opportunity for a book on redesigning work and got me enthusiastic about writing it in an improbably short period of time. Thank you also to Celia Buzuk at Penguin for her enthusiasm and constant support. Together they ensured the book is relevant and timely. And as always, a big thank you to my dear friend and literary agent, Caroline Michel of PFD.

Because the topic of this book is so timely, we all pushed to complete it – and that inevitably meant spending long hours in my study. I am very appreciative of the support of my husband Nigel Boardman and my boys Christian Seiersen and Dominic Seiersen.

Notes

Introduction

1 L. Gratton and A. J. Scott, *The 100-Year Life: Living and Working in an Age of Longevity* (Bloomsbury, 2016); A. J. Scott and L. Gratton, *The New Long Life: A Framework for Flourishing in a Changing World* (Bloomsbury, 2020).

2 K. Lewin, *Field Theory in Social Science: Selected Theoretical Papers*, ed. Dorwin Cartwright (Harper, 1951).

3 J. Rawls, *A Theory of Justice* (Harvard University Press, 1971).

4 US National Bureau of Economic Research, 'Away from home and back: coordinating (remote) workers in 1800 and 2020', NBER, December 2020.

5 N. Bloom, 'The productivity pitfalls of working from home in the age of Covid-19'. Interview by Adam Gorlick, *Stanford News*, 30 March 2020.

6 US National Bureau of Economic Research, 'Collaborating during Corona-virus: the impact of Covid-19 on the nature of work', NBER, July 2020.

7 A. Haldane, 'Does working from home make us more or less creative?', *Financial Times*, 26 October 2020.

8 L. Thompson, 'Virtual collaboration won't be the death of collaboration', *MIT Sloan Management Review*, 8 December 2020.

Chapter 2: Understand

1 M. Polanyi, *The Tacit Dimension* (University of Chicago Press, 2009).

2 M. Kilduff and W. Tsai, *Social Networks and Organizations* (Sage, 2003); R. S. Burt, 'The network structure of social capital', *Research in Organizational Behaviour* 22 (2000): 345–423.

3 L. Gratton, *Hot Spots: Why Some Companies Buzz with Energy and Innovation – and Others Don't* (Prentice Hall, 2017).

4 M. Granovetter, *Getting a Job: A Study of Contacts and Careers* (University of Chicago Press, 1974).

5 R. S. Burt, 'Structural holes and good ideas', *American Journal of Sociology* 110, 2 (2004): 349–99.

6 L. Gratton, 'Maslow's hierarchy of needs across three social groups', unpublished doctoral thesis, 1981.

7 L. Gratton, *The Shift: The Future of Work is Already Here* (HarperCollins, 2014).

8 J. Petriglieri, 'Couples that work: how dual-career couples make it work', *Harvard Business Review*, September–October 2019.

9 McKinsey & Company, 'Global survey: the state of AI in 2020'; World Economic Forum, 'The future of jobs report, 2020'.

10 L. Gratton and A. J. Scott, 'The corporate implications of longer lives', *MIT Sloan Management Review*, March 2017.

11 Kauffman Index of Entrepreneurial Activity, '2018 National report on early-stage entrepreneurship'.

12 B. Groysberg, *Chasing Stars: The Myth of Talent and the Portability of Performance* (Princeton University Press, 2012).

13 McKinsey Global Institute, 'A labor market that works: connecting talent with opportunity in the digital age', June 2015.

14 Kaiser Family Foundation/*New York Times*/CBS News poll of 1,002 non-employed US adults, December 2014.

Chapter 3: Reimagine

1 L. Gratton, and S. Ghoshal, 'Beyond best practice', *MIT Sloan Management Review*, April 2005.

2 V. Alexander, 'I've been designing offices for decades. Here's what I got wrong', *Fast Company*, July 2019.

3 E. Bernstein and B. Waber, 'The truth about open offices', *Harvard Business Review*, December 2019.

4 N. Bloom, J. Laing, J. Roberts and J. Ying, 'Does working from home work – evidence from a Chinese experiment', Stanford Business Working Paper no. 3109, March 2013.

5 T. Jones and L. Gratton, 'The third wave of virtual work', *Harvard Business Review*, January–February 2013.

6 J. Useem, 'The psychological benefits of commuting to work', *The Atlantic*, July–August 2021.

7 B. E. Ashforth, *Role Transitions in Organizational Life: An Identity-based Perspective* (Routledge, 2000).

8 B. E. Ashforth, G. E. Kreiner and M. Fugate, 'All in a day's work: boundaries and micro role transitions', *Academy of Management Review* 25 (2000): 472–91.

9 Ibid.

10 J. Cerrato and E. Cifre, 'Gender inequality in household chores and work–family conflict', *Frontiers of Psychology*, 3 August 2018. See also Gallup data – for example M. Brenan, 'Women still handle main household tasks in U.S.', *Politics*, 29 January 2020.

11 A. Rattan, 'When confronting a biased comment can increase your sense of belonging at work', *Harvard Business Review* digital article, 4 May 2018.

12 R. Putnam, *Bowling Alone: The Collapse and Revival of American Community* (Simon & Schuster, 2000).

13 D. Silver et al., 'Mastering the game of Go without human knowledge', *Nature* 550 (2017): 354–9.

14 For an overview of the impact of AI on work: T. Malone, 'How human-computer "superminds" are defining the future of work', *MIT Sloan Management Review*, June 2018; T. Malone, D. Rus and R. Laubacher, 'Artificial intelligence and the future of work', MIT Work of the Future research brief 17, December 2020. How this might play out with regard to automation: Digital/McKinsey, 'Driving impact at scale from automation and AI', February 2019. For a discussion of the basis of causality: J. Pearl, *Causality: Models, Reasoning and Inference* (Cambridge University Press, 2000).

15 C. Barnes and G. Spreitzer, 'Why sleep is a strategic resource', *MIT Sloan Management Review*, December 2014.

16 E. Bernstein, J. Shore and D. Lazer, 'Improving the rhythm of your collaboration', *MIT Sloan Management Review*, September 2019.

17 M. Csikszentmihalyi, *Flow: The Psychology of Optimal Experience* (Harper Perennial, 2008).

18 L. A. Perlow, 'The time famine: toward a sociology of work time', *Administrative Science Quarterly* 44, 1 (1999): 57–81.

19 Bernstein, Shore and Lazer, 'Improving the rhythm of your collaboration'.

20 A. Whillans, 'Time confetti and the broken promise of leisure', *Behavioral Scientist*, 7 October 2020.

21 A. Whillans, *Time Smart: How to Reclaim Your Time and Live a Happier Life* (Harvard Business Review Press, 2020).

22 Bernstein, Shore and Lazer, 'Improving the rhythm of your collaboration'.

23 Ibid.

24 L. Perlow, C. N. Hadley and E. Eun, 'Stop the meeting madness; how to free up time for meaningful work', *Harvard Business Review*, July–August 2017.

25 C. Newport, *A World Without Email: Reimagining Work in an Age of Communication Overload* (Portfolio, 2021), and see also his 'Knowledge workers are bad at working (and here's what to do about it)', Study Hacks blog post, November 2012.

26 Microsoft White Paper, 'The new future of work: research from Microsoft into the pandemic's impact on work practices'.

27 T. Neeley, 'How to have a good meeting', *New York Times*, 25 June 2021.

28 C. Weaver, 'Meetings. Why? Does this conversation need to be a meeting? Does anything?', *New York Times*, 24 June 2021.

29 N. Bloom, J. Davis and Z. Zhestkova, 'COVID-19 shifted patent applications towards technologies that support working from home', Becker Friedman Institute Working Paper no. 2020-133, January 2021.

30 Samantha Schaevitz, 'Three months, 30x demand: how we scaled Google Meet during COVID-19', Google Workspace, 6 August 2020.

31 C. Baden-Fuller and S. Haefliger, 'Business models and technological innovation', *Long Range Planning* 46, 6 (2013): 419–26.

32 E. Bernstein, *A Manager's Guide to the New World of Work: The Most Effective Strategies for Managing People, Teams and Organizations* (MIT Press, 2020).

33 Simon Read, 'No full-time return to the office for over a million', BBC News, 6 May 2021.

Chapter 4: Model and Test

1 Scott and Gratton, *The New Long Life*.

2 A. J. Scott, M. Ellison and D. A. Sinclair, 'The economic value of targeting aging', *Nature Aging* 1 (2021): 616–23.

3 J. Hartshorne and L. Germine, 'When does cognitive functioning peak? The asynchronous rise and fall of cognitive abilities across the life span', *Psychological Science* 26, 4 (2015): 433–43.

4 Roleshare podcast, 'Don't choose between the best talent – get both', 15 October 2020; www.roleshare.com/toolkit/dont-choose-between-the-best-talent-get-both.

5 'The Job Share Project – job-sharing at senior levels – making it work', report by Capability Jane 2020; https://thejobshareproject.com/.

6 Civil Service people survey 2018, results by demographic group.

7 PwC, 'Hopes and fears 2021 – the view of 32,500 workers'.

8 World Economic Forum, 'The future of jobs report 2020'.

9 D. Autor, 'Why are there still so many jobs? – The history and future of workplace automation', *Journal of Economic Perspectives* 29, 3 (2015): 3–30.

10 D. Autor, D. Mindell and E. Reynolds, 'The work of the future – building better jobs in an age of intelligent machines', report by MIT's task force on the future of work, November 2020.

11 Ibid.

12 World Economic Forum, 'The future of jobs report – employment, skills and workforce strategy for the Fourth Industrial Revolution', January 2016.

13 L. Gratton, 'The challenge of scaling soft skills', *MIT Sloan Management Review*, August 2018.

14 S. Turkle, *Alone Together: Why We Expect More from Technology and Less from Each Other* (Basic Books, 2017).

15 L. Gratton, 'An emerging landscape of skills for all', *MIT Sloan Management Review*, March 2021.

16 P. Blair et al., 'Search for STARs: work experience as a job market signal for workers without a bachelor's degree', NFER Working Paper Series 26844, and 'Reach for the STARs: the potential of America's hidden talent pool', Opportunity@Work and Accenture, March 2020.

17 L. Gratton, *The Key: How Corporations Succeed by Solving the World's Toughest Problems* (McGraw-Hill, 2014).

18 World Economic Forum Global Council on the New Agenda for Work, Wages and Job Creation, *Building Back Broader: Policy Pathways for an Economic Transformation*, White Paper, June 2021.

19 P. Zac, 'The neuroscience of trust – management behaviours that foster employee engagement', *Harvard Business Review*, January–February 2017.

20 J. Brockner, 'Why it's so hard to be fair', *Harvard Business Review*, March 2006.

21 J. Greenberg and J. Colquitt (eds), *Handbook of Organizational Justice* (Psychology Press, 2005).

22 Edelman 2020 Trust Barometer; www.edelman.com/trust/2020-trust-barometer.

23 M. Sverke, J. Hellgren and K. Näswall (2002), 'No security: a meta-analysis and review of job insecurity and its consequences', *Journal of Occupational Health Psychology* 7 (2002): 242–64; see also S. J. Sucher and S. Gupta, 'Layoffs that don't break your company: better approaches to workforce transition', *Harvard Business Review*, May–June 2018.

Chapter 5: Act and Create

1 H. Mintzberg, *The Nature of Managerial Work* (Harper & Row, 1973).

2 WTI Pulse Report, 'In hybrid work, managers keep teams connected', Microsoft, 2021; www.microsoft.com/en-us/worklab/work-trend-index/managers-keep-teams-connected.

3 C. C. Markides, *Organizing for the New Normal: Preparing Your Company for the Journey of Continuous Disruption* (Kogan Page, 2021).

4 A. Hill, 'It's time to extinguish the "burning platform" for good', *Financial Times*, 27 June 2021.

5 J. Hagel, *The Journey Beyond Fear: Leverage the Three Pillars of Positivity to Build Your Success* (McGraw-Hill, 2021).

6 Ibid.

7 H. Chesbrough, 'The era of open innovation', *MIT Sloan Management Review*, April 2003.

8 P. J. Zak, 'Why your brain loves good storytelling', *Harvard Business Review*, 28 October 2014.

9 S. Friedman, *Leading the Life You Want: Integrating Work and Life* (Harvard Business Review Press, 2014).

Index

PENGUIN PARTNERSHIPS

Penguin Partnerships is the Creative Sales and Promotions team at Penguin Random House. We have a long history of working with clients on a wide variety of briefs, specializing in brand promotions, bespoke publishing and retail exclusives, plus corporate, entertainment and media partnerships.

We can respond quickly to briefs and specialize in repurposing books and content for sales promotions, for use as incentives and retail exclusives as well as creating content for new books in collaboration with our partners as part of branded book relationships.

Equally if you'd simply like to buy a bulk quantity of one of our existing books at a special discount, we can help with that too. Our books can make excellent corporate or employee gifts.

Special editions, including personalized covers, excerpts of existing books or books with corporate logos can be created in large quantities for special needs.

We can work within your budget to deliver whatever you want, however you want it.

For more information, please contact
salesenquiries@penguinrandomhouse.co.uk